T0261385

Ethernet Switches

Charles E. Spurgeon and Joann Zimmerman

O'REILLY®

Beijing · Cambridge · Farnham · Köln · Sebastopol · Tokyo

Ethernet Switches

by Charles E. Spurgeon and Joann Zimmerman

Copyright © 2013 Charles Spurgeon and Joann Zimmerman. All rights reserved.

Printed in the United States of America.

Published by O'Reilly Media, Inc., 1005 Gravenstein Highway North, Sebastopol, CA 95472.

O'Reilly books may be purchased for educational, business, or sales promotional use. Online editions are also available for most titles (*http://my.safaribooksonline.com*). For more information, contact our corporate/institutional sales department: 800-998-9938 or *corporate@oreilly.com*.

Editor: Meghan Blanchette	**Cover Designer:** Randy Comer
Production Editor: Marisa LaFleur	**Interior Designer:** David Futato
Proofreader: Marisa LaFleur	**Illustrator:** Rebecca Demarest

April 2013:   First Edition

Revision History for the First Edition:

2013-03-29:   First release

See *http://oreilly.com/catalog/errata.csp?isbn=9781449367305* for release details.

Nutshell Handbook, the Nutshell Handbook logo, and the O'Reilly logo are registered trademarks of O'Reilly Media, Inc. *Ethernet Switches*, the image of a Common Cuttlefish, and related trade dress are trademarks of O'Reilly Media, Inc.

Many of the designations used by manufacturers and sellers to distinguish their products are claimed as trademarks. Where those designations appear in this book, and O'Reilly Media, Inc., was aware of a trademark claim, the designations have been printed in caps or initial caps.

While every precaution has been taken in the preparation of this book, the publisher and authors assume no responsibility for errors or omissions, or for damages resulting from the use of the information contained herein.

ISBN: 978-1-449-36730-5

[LSI]

Table of Contents

Preface

Ethernet switches, also known as bridges, are basic building blocks of networks, and are so commonly used that you may not give them a second thought. It's possible to build networks without knowing very much about how switches work. However, when you build larger network systems, it helps to understand both what goes on inside a switch and how the standards make it possible for switches to work together.

Ethernet is used to build networks from small to large, and from simple to complex. Ethernet connects your home computers and other household devices; switches for home networks are typically small, low cost, and simple. Ethernet also connects the Internet worldwide, and switches for Internet Service Providers are large, high cost, and complex.

Campus and enterprise networks often use a mix of switches: simpler and lower-cost switches are usually found inside wiring closets and used to connect devices on a given floor of a building; larger and higher-cost switches are found in the core of the network and are used to connect all the building switches together into a larger network system. Data center networks have their own special requirements, and typically include high performance switches that can be connected in ways that provide highly resilient networks.

According to industry estimates, the worldwide market for enterprise switches recorded revenues of over $5 billion per quarter in 2012, with total revenues exceeding $20 billion for the year. For the second quarter of 2012, there were 55 million Gigabit Ethernet ports shipped, and 3 million 10-Gigabit ports. At that rate, over 230 million enterprise switch ports were sold in 2012. Aside from the enterprise market, there were annual revenues of roughly $14 billion for service provider switches, resulting in total Ethernet switch revenues of roughly $34 billion for 2012. To satisfy the large and ever-increasing market for Ethernet switches, there are many varieties of switches offered at many price points.

The many kinds of switches and the many features that can be found in those switches are both very extensive topics. Covering the entire range of technology and the various ways switches can be used in network designs would require an entire book, or even several books. Instead, we will provide an introduction and a brief tutorial on how switches function, as well as how they are used in network designs. We will also provide an overview of the most important features found in switches—from the basics, to the more advanced features found in higher-cost and specialized switches.

Figure P-1 shows the topics discussed in this guide. Chapter 1 provides a tutorial on basic switch operation and the spanning tree protocol. In Chapter 2, we look at the management of switches, and at some of the most widely used switch features. Chapter 3 describes the advantages of switches in network designs, and how implementing a hierarchical network design can help maintain stable operations. Chapter 4 looks at the development of specialized switches to meet the more complex requirements of large networks, data center networks, and Internet Service Providers, while Chapter 5 describes some advanced switch features. Appendix A lists resources for further information.

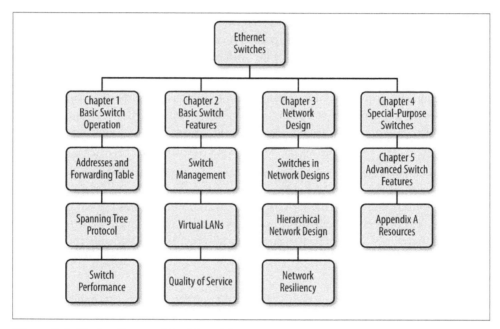

Figure P-1. Topics discussed in this guide

Conventions Used in This Book

The following typographical conventions are used in this book:

Italic
> Indicates new terms, URLs, email addresses, filenames, and file extensions.

Constant width

> Used for program listings, as well as within paragraphs to refer to program elements such as variable or function names, databases, data types, environment variables, statements, and keywords.

Constant width bold

> Shows commands or other text that should be typed literally by the user.

Constant width italic

> Shows text that should be replaced with user-supplied values or by values determined by context.

 This icon signifies a tip, suggestion, or general note.

 This icon indicates a warning or caution.

Using Code Examples

This book is here to help you get your job done. In general, if this book includes code examples, you may use the code in this book in your programs and documentation. You do not need to contact us for permission unless you're reproducing a significant portion of the code. For example, writing a program that uses several chunks of code from this book does not require permission. Selling or distributing a CD-ROM of examples from O'Reilly books does require permission. Answering a question by citing this book and quoting example code does not require permission. Incorporating a significant amount of example code from this book into your product's documentation does require permission.

We appreciate, but do not require, attribution. An attribution usually includes the title, author, publisher, and ISBN. For example: *Ethernet Switches* by Charles E. Spurgeon and Joann Zimmerman (O'Reilly). Copyright 2013 Charles E. Spurgeon and Joann Zimmerman, 978-1-449-36730-5.

If you feel your use of code examples falls outside fair use or the permission given above, feel free to contact us at *permissions@oreilly.com*.

Safari® Books Online

 *Safari Books Online* is an on-demand digital library that delivers expert content in both book and video form from the world's leading authors in technology and business.

Technology professionals, software developers, web designers, and business and creative professionals use Safari Books Online as their primary resource for research, problem solving, learning, and certification training.

Safari Books Online offers a range of product mixes and pricing programs for organizations, government agencies, and individuals. Subscribers have access to thousands of books, training videos, and prepublication manuscripts in one fully searchable database from publishers like O'Reilly Media, Prentice Hall Professional, Addison-Wesley Professional, Microsoft Press, Sams, Que, Peachpit Press, Focal Press, Cisco Press, John Wiley & Sons, Syngress, Morgan Kaufmann, IBM Redbooks, Packt, Adobe Press, FT Press, Apress, Manning, New Riders, McGraw-Hill, Jones & Bartlett, Course Technology, and dozens more. For more information about Safari Books Online, please visit us online.

How to Contact Us

Please address comments and questions concerning this book to the publisher:

O'Reilly Media, Inc.
1005 Gravenstein Highway North
Sebastopol, CA 95472
800-998-9938 (in the United States or Canada)
707-829-0515 (international or local)
707-829-0104 (fax)

We have a web page for this book, where we list errata, examples, and any additional information. You can access this page at *http://oreil.ly/ethernetswitches*.

To comment or ask technical questions about this book, send email to *bookques tions@oreilly.com*.

For more information about our books, courses, conferences, and news, see our website at *http://www.oreilly.com*.

Find us on Facebook: *http://facebook.com/oreilly*

Follow us on Twitter: *http://twitter.com/oreillymedia*

Watch us on YouTube: *http://www.youtube.com/oreillymedia*

Acknowledgements

The authors would like to thank Rich Seifert, author of *The Switch Book* (Wiley), and a participant on Ethernet standards committees, for his technical review and valuable comments. Of course, we are responsible for any remaining errors. Please use the contact information above to provide comments or corrections.

CHAPTER 1

Basic Switch Operation

What an Ethernet Switch Does

Ethernet switches link Ethernet devices together by relaying Ethernet *frames* between the devices connected to the switches. By moving Ethernet frames between the switch *ports*, a switch links the traffic carried by the individual network connections into a larger Ethernet network.

Ethernet switches perform their linking function by *bridging* Ethernet frames between Ethernet *segments*. To do this, they copy Ethernet frames from one switch port to another, based on the *Media Access Control (MAC)* addresses in the Ethernet frames. Ethernet bridging was initially defined in the 802.1D IEEE Standard for Local and Metropolitan Area Networks: Media Access Control (MAC) Bridges (*http://bit.ly/ieee-standards*).[1]

The standardization of bridging operations in switches makes it possible to buy switches from different vendors that will work together when combined in a network design. That's the result of lots of hard work on the part of the standards engineers to define a set of standards that vendors could agree upon and implement in their switch designs.

Bridges and Switches

The first Ethernet bridges were two-port devices that could link two of the original Ethernet system's coaxial cable segments together. At that time, Ethernet only supported connections to coaxial cables. Later, when twisted-pair Ethernet was developed and switches with many ports became widely available, they were often used as the central

---

1. The most recent version of the 802.1D bridging standard is dated 2004. The 802.1D standard was extended and enhanced by the subsequent development of the 802.1Q-2011 standard, "Media Access Control (MAC) Bridges and Virtual Bridge Local Area Networks."

connection point, or hub, of Ethernet cabling systems, resulting in the name "switching hub." Today, in the marketplace, these devices are simply called switches.

Things have changed quite a lot since Ethernet bridges were first developed in the early 1980s. Over the years, computers have become ubiquitous, and many people use multiple devices at their jobs, including their laptops, smartphones, and tablets. Every VoIP telephone and every printer is a computer, and even building management systems and access controls (door locks) are networked. Modern buildings have multiple wireless access points (APs) to provide 802.11 Wi-Fi services for things like smartphones and tablets, and each of the APs is also connected to a cabled Ethernet system. As a result, modern Ethernet networks may consist of hundreds of switch connections in a building, and thousands of switch connections across a campus network.

What Is a Switch?

You should know that there is another network device used to link networks, called a *router*. There are major differences in the ways that bridges and routers work, and they both have advantages and disadvantages, as described in "Routers or Bridges?" on page 42. Very briefly, bridges move frames between Ethernet segments based on Ethernet addresses with little or no configuration of the bridge required. Routers move *packets* between networks based on high-level protocol addresses, and each network being linked must be configured into the router. However, both bridges and routers are used to build larger networks, and both devices are called switches in the marketplace.

 We will use the words "bridge" and "switch" interchangeably to describe Ethernet bridges. However, note that "switch" is a generic term for network devices that may function as bridges, or routers, or even both, depending on their feature sets and configuration. The point is that as far as network experts are concerned, bridging and routing are different kinds of packet switching with different capabilities. For our purposes, we will follow the practices of Ethernet vendors who use the word "switch," or more specifically, "Ethernet switch," to describe devices that bridge Ethernet frames.

While the 802.1D standard provides the specifications for bridging local area network frames between ports of a switch, and for a few other aspects of basic bridge operation, the standard is also careful to avoid specifying issues like bridge or switch performance or how switches should be built. Instead, vendors compete with one another to provide switches at multiple price points and with multiple levels of performance and capabilities.

The result has been a large and competitive market in Ethernet switches, increasing the number of choices you have as a customer. The wide range of switch models and capabilities can be confusing. In Chapter 4, we discuss special purpose switches and their uses.

Operation of Ethernet Switches

Networks exist to move data between computers. To perform that task, the network software organizes the data being moved into Ethernet frames. Frames travel over Ethernet networks, and the data field of a frame is used to carry data between computers. Frames are nothing more than arbitrary sequences of information whose format is defined in a standard.

The format for an Ethernet frame includes a destination *address* at the beginning, containing the address of the device to which the frame is being sent.[2] Next comes a source address, containing the address of the device sending the frame. The addresses are followed by various other fields, including the data field that carries the data being sent between computers, as shown in Figure 1-1.

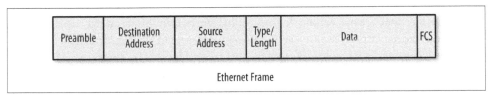

Figure 1-1. Ethernet frame format

Frames are defined at Layer 2, or the *Data Link Layer*, of the *Open Systems Interconnection (OSI)* seven-layer network model. The seven-layer model was developed to organize the kinds of information sent between computers. It is used to define how that information will be sent and to structure the development of standards for transferring information. Since Ethernet switches operate on local area network frames at the Data Link Layer, you will sometimes hear them called link layer devices, as well as Layer 2 devices or Layer 2 switches.[3]

2. The Preamble field at the beginning of the frame is automatically stripped off when the frame is received on an Ethernet interface, leaving the Destination Address as the first field.

3. The TCP/IP network protocol is based on network layer *packets*. The TCP/IP packets are carried between computers in the data field of Ethernet frames. In essence, Ethernet functions as the trucking system that transports TCP/IP packets between computers, carried as data in the Ethernet frame. You will also hear Ethernet frames referred to as "packets," but as far as the standards are concerned, Ethernet uses frames to carry data between computers.

Transparent Bridging

Ethernet switches are designed so that their operations are invisible to the devices on the network, which explains why this approach to linking networks is also called *transparent bridging*. "Transparent" means that when you connect a switch to an Ethernet system, no changes are made in the Ethernet frames that are bridged. The switch will automatically begin working without requiring any configuration on the switch or any changes on the part of the computers connected to the Ethernet network, making the operation of the switch transparent to them.

Next, we will look at the basic functions used in a bridge to make it possible to forward Ethernet frames from one port to another.

Address Learning

An Ethernet switch controls the transmission of frames between switch ports connected to Ethernet cables using the traffic *forwarding* rules described in the IEEE 802.1D bridging standard. Traffic forwarding is based on address learning. Switches make traffic forwarding decisions based on the 48-bit media access control (MAC) addresses used in LAN standards, including Ethernet.

To do this, the switch learns which devices, called *stations* in the standard, are on which segments of the network by looking at the source addresses in all of the frames it receives. When an Ethernet device sends a frame, it puts two addresses in the frame. These two addresses are the *destination* address of the device it is sending the frame to, and the *source* address, which is the address of the device sending the frame.

The way the switch "learns" is fairly simple. Like all Ethernet interfaces, every port on a switch has a unique factory-assigned *MAC address*. However, unlike a normal Ethernet device that accepts only frames addressed directed to it, the Ethernet interface located in each port of a switch runs in *promiscuous* mode. In this mode, the interface is programmed to receive *all* frames it sees on that port, not just the frames that are being sent to the MAC address of the Ethernet interface on that switch port.

As each frame is received on each port, the switching software looks at the source address of the frame and adds that source address to a table of addresses that the switch maintains. This is how the switch automatically discovers which stations are reachable on which ports.

Figure 1-2 shows a switch linking six Ethernet devices. For convenience, we're using short numbers for station addresses, instead of actual 6-byte MAC addresses. As stations send traffic, the switch receives every frame sent and builds a table, more formally called a *forwarding database*, that shows which stations can be reached on which ports. After every station has transmitted at least one frame, the switch will end up with a forwarding database such as that shown in Table 1-1.

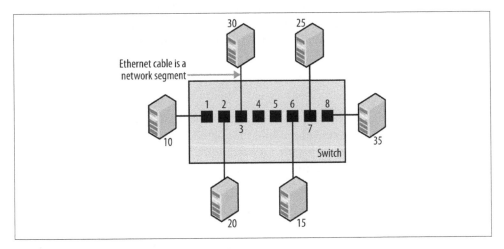

Figure 1-2. Address learning in a switch

Table 1-1. Forwarding database maintained by a switch

Port	Station
1	10
2	20
3	30
4	No station
5	No station
6	15
7	25
8	35

This database is used by the switch to make a packet forwarding decision in a process called *adaptive filtering*. Without an address database, the switch would have to send traffic received on any given port out all other ports to ensure that it reached its destination. With the address database, the traffic is filtered according to its destination. The switch is "adaptive" by learning new addresses automatically. This ability to learn makes it possible for you to add new stations to your network without having to manually configure the switch to know about the new stations, or the stations to know about the switch.[4]

---

4. Any Ethernet system still using coaxial cable segments and/or repeater hubs may have multiple stations on a network segment. Connecting that segment to a switch will result in multiple stations being reachable over a single port.

When the switch receives a frame that is destined for a station address that it hasn't yet seen, the switch will send the frame out all of the ports other than the port on which it arrived.[5] This process is called *flooding*, and is explained in more detail later in "Frame Flooding" on page 7.

Traffic Filtering

Once the switch has built a database of addresses, it has all the information it needs to filter and forward traffic selectively. While the switch is learning addresses, it is also checking each frame to make a packet forwarding decision based on the destination address in the frame. Let's look at how the forwarding decision works in a switch equipped with eight ports, as shown in Figure 1-2.

Assume that a frame is sent from station 15 to station 20. Since the frame is sent by station 15, the switch reads the frame in on port 6 and uses its address database to determine which of its ports is associated with the destination address in this frame. Here, the destination address corresponds to station 20, and the address database shows that to reach station 20, the frame must be sent out port 2.

Each port in the switch has the ability to hold frames in memory, before transmitting them onto the Ethernet cable connected to the port. For example, if the port is already busy transmitting when a frame arrives for transmission, then the frame can be held for the short time it takes for the port to complete transmitting the previous frame. To transmit the frame, the switch places the frame into the packet switching queue for transmission on port 2.

During this process, a switch transmitting an Ethernet frame from one port to another makes no changes to the data, addresses, or other fields of the basic Ethernet frame. Using our example, the frame is transmitted intact on port 2 exactly as it was received on port 6. Therefore, the operation of the switch is transparent to all stations on the network.

Note that the switch will not forward a frame destined for a station that is in the forwarding database onto a port unless that port is connected to the target destination. In other words, traffic destined for a device on a given port will only be sent to that port; no other ports will see the traffic intended for that device. This switching logic keeps traffic isolated to only those Ethernet cables, or segments, needed to receive the frame from the sender and transmit that frame to the destination device.

---

5. Suppressing frame transmission on the switch port prevents stations on a shared segment connected to that port from seeing the same traffic more than once. This also prevents a single station on a port from receiving a copy of the frame it just sent.

This prevents the flow of unnecessary traffic on other segments of the network system, which is a major advantage of a switch. This is in contrast to the early Ethernet system, where traffic from any station was seen by all other stations, whether they wanted the data or not. Switch traffic filtering reduces the traffic load carried by the set of Ethernet cables connected to the switch, thereby making more efficient use of the network bandwidth.

Frame Flooding

Switches automatically age out entries in their forwarding database after a period of time—typically five minutes—if they do not see any frames from a station. Therefore, if a station doesn't send traffic for a designated period, then the switch will delete the forwarding entry for that station. This keeps the forwarding database from growing full of stale entries that might not reflect reality.

Of course, once the address entry has timed out, the switch won't have any information in the database for that station the next time the switch receives a frame destined for it. This also happens when a station is newly connected to a switch, or when a station has been powered off and is turned back on more than five minutes later. So how does the switch handle packet forwarding for an unknown station?

The solution is simple: the switch forwards the frame destined for an unknown station out all switch ports other than the one it was received on, thus *flooding* the frame to all other stations. Flooding the frame guarantees that a frame with an unknown destination address will reach all network connections and be heard by the correct destination device, assuming that it is active and on the network. When the unknown device responds with return traffic, the switch will automatically learn which port the device is on, and will no longer flood traffic destined to that device.

Broadcast and Multicast Traffic

In addition to transmitting frames directed to a single address, local area networks are capable of sending frames directed to a group address, called a *multicast address*, which can be received by a group of stations. They can also send frames directed to all stations, using the *broadcast address*. Group addresses always begin with a specific bit pattern defined in the Ethernet standard, making it possible for a switch to determine which frames are destined for a specific device rather than a group of devices.

A frame sent to a multicast destination address can be received by all stations configured to listen for that multicast address. The Ethernet software, also called "interface driver" software, programs the interface to accept frames sent to the group address, so that the interface is now a member of that group. The Ethernet interface address assigned at the factory is called a *unicast* address, and any given Ethernet interface can receive unicast frames and multicast frames. In other words, the interface can be programmed to receive frames sent to one or more multicast group addresses, as well as frames sent to the unicast MAC address belonging to that interface.

Broadcast and multicast forwarding

The broadcast address is a special multicast group: the group of all of the stations in the network. A packet sent to the broadcast address (the address of all 1s) is received by every station on the LAN. Since broadcast packets must be received by all stations on the network, the switch will achieve that goal by flooding broadcast packets out all ports except the port that it was received on, since there's no need to send the packet back to the originating device. This way, a broadcast packet sent by any station will reach all other stations on the LAN.

Multicast traffic can be more difficult to deal with than broadcast frames. More sophisticated (and usually more expensive) switches include support for multicast group discovery protocols that make it possible for each station to tell the switch about the multicast group addresses that it wants to hear, so the switch will send the multicast packets only to the ports connected to stations that have indicated their interest in receiving the multicast traffic. However, lower cost switches, with no capability to discover which ports are connected to stations listening to a given multicast address, must resort to flooding multicast packets out all ports other than the port on which the multicast traffic was received, just like broadcast packets.

Uses of broadcast and multicast

Stations send broadcast and multicast packets for a number of reasons. High-level network protocols like TCP/IP use broadcast or multicast frames as part of their address discovery process. Broadcasts and multicasts are also used for dynamic address assignment, which occurs when a station is first powered on and needs to find a high-level network address. Multicasts are also used by certain multimedia applications, which send audio and video data in multicast frames for reception by groups of stations, and by multi-user games as a way of sending data to a group of game players.

Therefore, a typical network will have some level of broadcast and multicast traffic. As long as the number of such frames remains at a reasonable level, then there won't be any problems. However, when many stations are combined by switches into a single large network, broadcast and multicast flooding by the switches can result in significant amounts of traffic. Large amounts of broadcast or multicast traffic may cause network congestion, since every device on the network is required to receive and process broadcasts and specific types of multicasts; at high enough packet rates, there could be performance issues for the stations.

Streaming applications (video) sending high rates of multicasts can generate intense traffic. Disk backup and disk duplication systems based on multicast can also generate lots of traffic. If this traffic ends up being flooded to all ports, the network could congest.

One way to avoid this congestion is to limit the total number of stations linked to a single network, so that the broadcast and multicast rate does not get so high as to be a problem.

Another way to limit the rate of multicast and broadcast packets is to divide the network into multiple *virtual LANs (VLANs)*. Yet another method is to use a router, also called a Layer 3 switch. Since a router does not automatically forward broadcasts and multi-casts, this creates separate network systems.[6] These methods for controlling the propagation of multicasts and broadcasts are discussed in Chapter 2 and Chapter 3, respectively.

Combining Switches

So far we've seen how a single switch can forward traffic based on a dynamically-created forwarding database. A major difficulty with this simple model of switch operation is that multiple connections between switches can create loop paths, leading to network congestion and overload.

Forwarding Loops

The design and operation of Ethernet requires that only a single packet transmission path may exist between any two stations. An Ethernet grows by extending branches in a network *topology* called a tree structure, which consists of multiple switches branching off of a central switch. The danger is that, in a sufficiently complex network, switches with multiple inter-switch connections can create loop paths in the network.

On a network with switches connected together to form a packet forwarding loop, packets will circulate endlessly around the loop, building up to very high levels of traffic and causing an overload.

The looped packets will circulate at the maximum rate of the network links, until the traffic rate gets so high that the network is saturated. Broadcast and multicast frames, as well as unicast frames to unknown destinations, are normally flooded to all ports in a basic switch, and all of this traffic will circulate in such a loop. Once a loop is formed, this failure mode can happen very rapidly, causing the network to be fully occupied with sending broadcast, multicast, and unknown frames, and it becomes very difficult for stations to send actual traffic.

Unfortunately, loops like the dotted path shown with arrows in Figure 1-3 are all too easy to achieve, despite your best efforts to avoid them. As networks grow to include

---

6. Both Layer 3 networks and VLANs create separate *broadcast domains*. Broadcasts and link layer multicasts are not automatically forwarded between networks by routers, and each VLAN operates as a separate and distinct LAN. Therefore, both routers and VLANs provide separate broadcast domains that limit the prop-agation of broadcasts and multicasts in a complex network system.

more switches and more wiring closets, it becomes difficult to know exactly how things are connected together and to keep people from mistakenly creating a loop path.

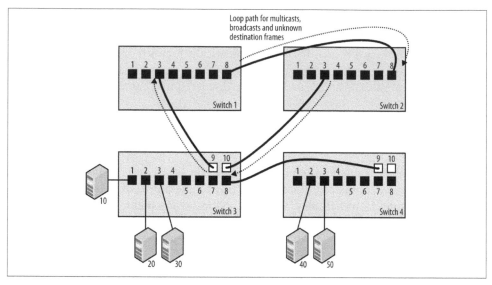

Figure 1-3. Forwarding loop between switches

While the loop in the drawing is intended to be obvious, in a sufficiently complex network system it can be challenging for anyone working on the network to know whether or not the switches are connected in such a way as to create loop paths. The IEEE 802.1D bridging standard provides a spanning tree protocol to avoid this problem by automatically suppressing forwarding loops.

Spanning Tree Protocol

The purpose of the *spanning tree protocol (STP)* is to allow switches to automatically create a loop-free set of paths, even in a complex network with multiple paths connecting multiple switches. It provides the ability to dynamically create a tree topology in a network by blocking any packet forwarding on certain ports, and ensures that a set of Ethernet switches can automatically configure themselves to produce loop-free paths. The IEEE 802.1D standard describes the operation of spanning tree, and every switch that claims compliance with the 802.1D standard must include spanning tree capability.[7]

---

7. Beware that low-cost switches may not include spanning tree capability, rendering them unable to block any packet forwarding loops. Also, some vendors that provide spanning tree may disable it by default, requiring you to manually enable spanning tree before it will function to protect your network.

Spanning Tree Packets

Operation of the spanning tree algorithm is based on configuration messages sent by each switch in packets called Bridge Protocol Data Units, or BPDUs. Each BPDU packet is sent to a destination multicast address that has been assigned to spanning tree operation. All IEEE 802.1D switches join the BPDU multicast group and listen to frames sent to this address, so that every switch can send and receive spanning tree configuration messages.[8]

Choosing a Root Bridge

The process of creating a spanning tree begins by using the information in the BPDU configuration messages to automatically elect a *root bridge*. The election is based on a bridge ID (BID) which, in turn, is based on the combination of a configurable bridge priority value (32,768 by default) and the unique Ethernet MAC address assigned on each bridge for use by the spanning tree process, called the system MAC. Bridges send BPDUs to one another, and the bridge with the lowest BID is automatically elected to be the root bridge.

Assuming that the bridge priority was left at the default value of 32,768, then the bridge with the lowest numerical value Ethernet address will be the one elected as the root bridge.[9] In the example shown in Figure 1-4, Switch 1 has the lowest BID, and the end result of the spanning tree election process is that Switch 1 has become the root bridge. Electing the root bridge sets the stage for the rest of the operations performed by the spanning tree protocol.

Choosing the Least-Cost Path

Once a root bridge is chosen, each non-root bridge uses that information to determine which of its ports has the least-cost path to the root bridge, then assigns that port to be the root port (RP). All other bridges determine which of their ports connected to other links has the least-cost path to the root bridge. The bridge with the least-cost path is assigned the role of designated bridge (DB), and the ports on the DB are assigned as designated ports (DP).

---

8. The bridge multicast group MAC address is 01-80-C2-00-00-00. Vendor-specific spanning tree enhancements may also use other addresses. For example, Cisco per-VLAN spanning tree (PVST) sends BPDUs to address 01-00-0C-CC-CC-CD.

9. It may happen that a low-performance bridge on your network will have the lowest MAC address and end up as the root bridge. You can configure a lower bridge priority on your core bridge to ensure that the core bridge is chosen to be the root, and that the root will be located at the core of your network and running on the higher-performance switch located there.

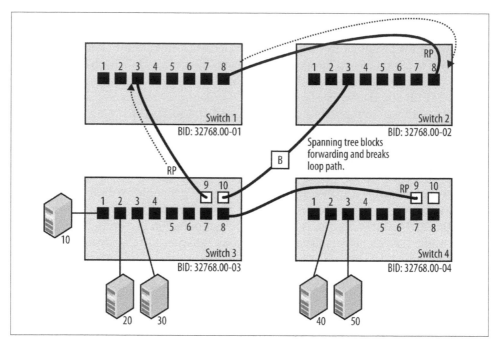

Figure 1-4. Spanning tree operation

The *path cost* is based on the speed at which the ports operate, with higher speeds resulting in lower costs. As BPDU packets travel through the system, they accumulate information about the number of ports they travel through and the speed of each port. Paths with slower speed ports will have higher costs. The total cost of a given path through multiple switches is the sum of the costs of all the ports on that path.

 If there are multiple paths to the root with the same cost, then the path connected to the bridge with the lowest bridge ID will be used.

At the end of this process, the bridges have chosen a set of root ports and designated ports, making it possible for the bridges to remove all loop paths and maintain a packet forwarding tree that spans the entire set of devices connected to the network, hence the name "spanning tree protocol."

Blocking Loop Paths

Once the spanning tree process has determined the port status, then the combination of root ports and designated ports provides the spanning tree algorithm with the information it needs to identify the best paths and block all other paths. Packet forwarding on any port that is not a root port or a designated port is disabled by *blocking* the forwarding of packets on that port.

While blocked ports do not forward packets, they continue to receive BPDUs. The blocked port is shown in Figure 1-4 with a "B," indicating that port 10 on Switch 3 is in blocking mode and that the link is not forwarding packets. *The Rapid Spanning Tree Protocol (RSTP)* sends BPDU packets every two seconds to monitor the state of the network, and a blocked port may become unblocked when a path change is detected.

Spanning Tree Port States

When an active device is connected to a switch port, the port goes through a number of states as it processes any BPDUs that it might receive, and the spanning tree process determines what state the port should be in at any given time. Two of the states are called *listening* and *learning*, during which the spanning tree process listens for BPDUs and also learns source addresses from any frames received.

Figure 1-5 shows the spanning tree port states, which include the following:

Disabled
> A port in this state has been intentionally shut down by an administrator, or has automatically shut down because the link was disconnected. This also could be a port that has failed, and is no longer operational. The Disabled state can be entered or exited from any other state.

Blocking
> A port that is enabled, but is not a root port or designated port could cause a switching loop if it were active. To avoid that, the port is placed in the blocking state. No station data is sent or received over a blocking port. Upon initialization of a port (link comes up, power is turned on), the port will typically enter the blocking state. Upon discovering via BPDUs or timeouts that the port may need to become active, the port will move to the listening state on the way to the forwarding state. A blocking port may also transition to the forwarding state if other links fail. BPDU data is still received while a port is in the blocking state.

Listening
> In this state, the port discards traffic but continues to process BPDUs received on the port, and acts on any new information that would cause the port to return to the blocked state. Based on information received in BPDUs, the port may transition to the learning state. The listening state allows the spanning tree algorithm to decide whether the attributes of this port, such as port cost, would cause the port to become part of the spanning tree or return to the blocking state.

Learning
> In this state, the port does not yet forward frames, but it does learn source addresses from any frames received and adds them to the filtering database. The switch will

populate the MAC address table with packets heard on the port (until the timer expires), before moving to the forwarding state.

Forwarding

This is the operational state in which a port sends and receives station data. Incoming BPDUs are also monitored to allow the bridge to detect if it needs to move the port into the blocking state to prevent a loop.

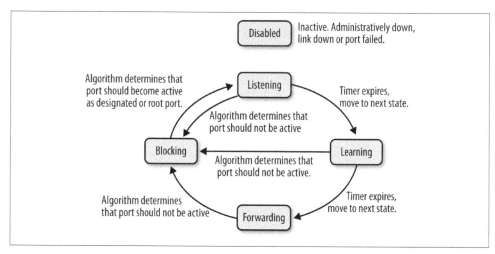

Figure 1-5. Spanning tree port states

In the original spanning tree protocol, the listening and learning states lasted for 30 seconds, during which time packets were not forwarded. In the newer Rapid Spanning Tree Protocol, it is possible to assign a port type of "edge" to a port, meaning that the port is known to be connected to an end station (user computer, VoIP telephone, printer, etc.) and not to another switch. That allows the RSTP state machine to bypass the learning and listening processes on that port and to transition to the forwarding state immediately. Allowing a station to immediately begin sending and receiving packets helps avoid such issues as application timeouts on user computers when they are rebooted.[10] While not required for RSTP operation, it is useful to manually configure RSTP edge ports with their port type, to avoid issues on user computers. Setting the port type to edge also means that RSTP doesn't need to send a BPDU packet upon link state change (link up or down) on that port, which helps reduce the amount of spanning tree traffic in the network.

---

10. Prior to the development of RSTP, some vendors had developed their own versions of this feature. Cisco Systems, for example, provided the "portfast" command to enable an edge port to immediately begin forwarding packets.

The inventor of the spanning tree protocol, Radia Perlman, wrote a poem to describe how it works.[11] When reading the poem it helps to know that in math terms, a network can be represented as a type of graph called a mesh, and that the goal of the spanning tree protocol is to turn any given network mesh into a tree structure with no loops that spans the entire set of network segments.

> I think that I shall never see
> A graph more lovely than a tree.
> A tree whose crucial property
> Is loop-free connectivity.
> A tree that must be sure to span
> So packets can reach every LAN.
> First, the root must be selected.
> By ID, it is elected.
> Least cost paths from root are traced.
> In the tree, these paths are placed.
> A mesh is made by folks like me,
> Then bridges find a spanning tree.
>
> — Radia Perlman
> *Algorhyme*

This brief description is only intended to provide the basic concepts behind the operation of the system. As you might expect, there are more details and complexities that are not described. The complete details of how the spanning tree state machine operates are described in the IEEE 802.1 standards, which can be consulted for a more complete understanding of the protocol and how it functions. The details of vendor-specific spanning tree enhancements can be found in the vendor documentation. See Appendix A for links to further information.

Spanning Tree Versions

The original spanning tree protocol, standardized in IEEE 802.1D, specified a single spanning tree process running on a switch, managing all ports and VLANs with a single spanning tree state machine. Nothing in the standard prohibits a vendor from developing their own enhancements to how spanning tree is deployed. Some vendors created their own implementations, in one case providing a separate spanning tree process per VLAN. That approach was taken by Cisco Systems for a version they call per-VLAN spanning tree (PVST).

---

11. Perlman, Radia. *Interconnections: Bridges, Routers, Switches and Internetworking Protocols (2nd Edition)*, New York: Addison-Wesley, 1999, p. 46.

The IEEE standard spanning tree protocol has evolved over the years. An updated version, called the Rapid Spanning Tree Protocol, was defined in 2004. As the name implies, Rapid Spanning Tree has increased the speed at which the protocol operates. RSTP was designed to provide backward compatibility with the original version of spanning tree. The 802.1Q standard includes both RSTP and a new version of spanning tree called Multiple Spanning Tree (MST), which is also designed to provide backward compatibility with previous versions.[12] MST is discussed further in "Virtual LANs" on page 26.

When building a network with multiple switches, you need to pay careful attention to how the vendor of your switches has deployed spanning tree, and to the version of spanning tree your switches use. The most commonly used versions, classic STP and the newer RSTP, are interoperable and require no configuration, resulting in "plug and play" operation.

Before putting a new switch into operation on your network, read the vendor's documentation carefully and make sure that you understand how things work. Some vendors may not enable spanning tree as a default on all ports. Other vendors may implement special features or vendor-specific versions of spanning tree. Typically, a vendor will work hard to make sure that their implementation of spanning tree "just works" with all other switches, but there are enough variations in spanning tree features and configuration that you may encounter issues. Reading the documentation and testing new switches before deploying them throughout your network can help avoid any problems.

Switch Performance Issues

A single *full-duplex* Ethernet connection is designed to move Ethernet frames between the Ethernet interfaces at each end of the connection. It operates at a known bit rate and a known maximum frame rate.[13] All Ethernet connections at a given speed will have the same bit rate and frame rate characteristics. However, adding switches to the network creates a more complex system. Now, the performance limits of your network become a combination of the performance of the Ethernet connections and the performance of the switches, as well as of any congestion that may occur in the system, depending on topology. It's up to you to make sure that the switches you buy have enough performance to do the job.

The performance of the internal switching electronics may not be able to sustain the full frame rate coming in from all ports. In other words, should all ports simultaneously present high traffic loads to the switch that are also continual and not just short bursts,

---

12. The IEEE 802.1Q standard notes that: "The spanning tree protocols specified by this standard supersede the Spanning Tree Protocol (STP) specified in IEEE Std 802.1D revisions prior to 2004, but facilitate migration by interoperating with the latter..."

13. For example, a 100 Mbps Ethernet LAN can send a maximum of 148,809 frames per second, when using the minimum frame size of 64 bytes.

the switch may not be able to handle the combined traffic rate and may begin dropping frames. This is known as *blocking*, the condition in a switching system in which there are insufficient resources available to provide for the flow of data through the switch. A *non-blocking switch* is one that provides enough internal switching capability to handle the full load even when all ports are simultaneously active for long periods of time. However, even a non-blocking switch will discard frames when a port becomes congested, depending on traffic patterns.

Packet Forwarding Performance

Typical switch hardware has dedicated support circuits that are designed to help improve the speed with which the switch can forward a frame and perform such essential functions as looking up frame addresses in the address filtering database. Because support circuits and high-speed buffer memory are more expensive components, the total performance of a switch is a trade-off between the cost of those high performance components and the price most customers are willing to pay. Therefore, you will find that not all switches perform alike.

Some less expensive devices may have lower packet forwarding performance, smaller address filtering tables, and smaller buffer memories. Larger switches with more ports will typically have higher performance components and a higher price tag. Switches capable of handling the maximum frame rate on all of their ports, also described as non-blocking switches, are capable of operating at *wire speed*. Fully non-blocking switches that can handle the maximum bit rate simultaneously on all ports are common these days, but it's always a good idea to check the specifications for the switch you are considering.

The performance required and the cost of the switches you purchase can vary depending on their location in the network. The switches you use in the core of a network need to have enough resources to handle high traffic loads. That's because the core of the network is where the traffic from all stations on the network converges. Core switches need to have the resources to handle multiple conversations, high traffic loads, and long duration traffic. On the other hand, the switches used at the edges of a network can be lower performance, since they are only required to handle the traffic loads of the directly connected stations.

Switch Port Memory

All switches contain some high-speed buffer memory in which a frame is stored, however briefly, before being forwarded onto another port or ports of the switch. This mechanism is known as *store-and-forward switching*. All IEEE 802.1D-compliant switches operate in store-and-forward mode, in which the packet is fully received on a port and placed into high-speed port buffer memory (stored) before being forwarded. A larger amount of buffer memory allows a bridge to handle longer streams of back-to-back frames, giving the switch improved performance in the presence of bursts of traffic on the LAN. A common switch design includes a pool of high-speed buffer memory that can be dynamically allocated to individual switch ports as needed.

Switch CPU and RAM

Given that a switch is a special-purpose computer, the central CPU and RAM in a switch are important for such functions as spanning tree operations, providing *management information*, managing multicast packet flows, and managing switch port and feature configuration.

As usual in the computer industry, the more CPU performance and RAM, the better, but you will pay more as well. Vendors frequently do not make it easy for customers to find switch CPU and RAM specifications. Typically, higher cost switches will make this information available, but you won't be able to order a faster CPU or more RAM for a given switch. Instead, this is information useful for comparing models from a vendor, or among vendors, to see which switches have the best specifications.

Switch Specifications

Switch performance includes a range of metrics, including the maximum bandwidth, or switching capacity of the packet switch electronics, inside the switch. You should also see the maximum number of MAC addresses that the address database can hold, as well as the maximum rate in packets per second that the switch can forward on the combined set of ports.

Shown here is a set of switch specifications copied from a typical vendor's data sheet. The vendor's specifications are shown in bold type. To keep things simple, in our example we show the specifications for a small, low-cost switch with five ports. This is intended to show you some typical switch values, and also to help you understand what the values mean and what happens when marketing and specifications meet on a single page.

Forwarding
  Store-and-forward
      Refers to standard 802.1D bridging, in which a packet is completely received on a port and into the port buffer ("store") before being forwarded.

  128 KB on-chip packet buffering
      The total amount of packet buffering available to all ports. The buffering is shared between the ports on an on-demand basis. This is a typical level of buffering for a small, light-duty, five-port switch intended to support client connections in a home office.

Some switches designed for use in data centers and other specialized networks support a mode of operation called *cut-through switching*, in which the packet forwarding process begins before the entire packet is read into buffer memory. The goal is to reduce the time required to forward a packet through the switch. This method also forwards packets with errors, since it begins forwarding a packet before the error checking field is received.

Performance
Bandwidth: 10 Gb/s (non-blocking)

Since this switch can handle the full traffic load across all ports operating at maximum traffic rate on each port, it is a non-blocking switch. The five ports can operate up to 1 Gb/s each. In *full-duplex mode*, the maximum rate through the switch, with all ports active, is 5 Gb/s in the outbound direction (also called "egress") and 5 Gb/s in the inbound direction (also called "ingress"). Vendors like to list a total of 10 Gb/s aggregate bandwidth on their specifications, although the 5 Gb/s of ingress data on five ports is being sent as 5 Gb/s of egress data. If you regarded the maximum aggregate data transfer through the switch as 5 Gb/s, you would be technically correct, but you would not succeed in marketing.[14]

Forwarding rate
10 Mbps port: 14,800 packets/sec
100 Mbps port: 148,800 packets/sec
1000 Mbps port: 1,480,000 packets/sec

These specifications show that the ports can handle the full packet switching rate consisting of minimum-sized Ethernet frames (64 bytes), which is as fast as the packet rate can go at the smallest frame size. Larger frames will have a lower packet rate per second, so this is the peak performance specification for an Ethernet switch. This shows that the switch can support the maximum packet rate on all ports at all supported speeds.

Latency (using 1500-byte packets)
10 Mbps: 30 microseconds (max)
100 Mbps: 6 microseconds (max)
1000 Mbps: 4 microseconds (max)

This is the amount of time it takes to move an Ethernet frame from the receiving port to the transmitting port, assuming that the transmitting port is available and not busy transmitting some other frame. It is a measure of the internal

14. If switch vendors marketed automobiles, then presumably they would market a car with a speedometer topping out at 120 mph as being a vehicle that provides an aggregate speed of 480 mph, since each of the four wheels can reach 120 mph at the same time. This is known as "marketing math" in the network marketplace.

switching delay imposed by the switch electronics. This measurement is also shown as 30 μs, using the Greek "mu" character to indicate "micro." A microsecond is one millionth of a second, and 30 millionths of a second latency on 10Mbps ports is a reasonable value for a low-cost switch. When comparing switches, a lower value is better. More expensive switches typically provide lower latency.

MAC address database: 4,000
This switch can support up to 4,000 unique station addresses in its address database. This is more than enough for a five-port switch intended for home office and small office use.

Mean time between failures
(MTBF): >1 million hours (~114 years) The MTBF is high because this switch is small, has no fan that can wear out, and has a low component count; there aren't many elements that can fail. This doesn't mean that the switch can't fail, but there are few failures in these electronics, resulting in a large mean time between failures for this switch design.

Standards compliance
IEEE 802.3i 10BASE-T Ethernet
IEEE 802.3u 100BASE-TX Fast Ethernet
IEEE 802.3ab 1000BASE-T Gigabit Ethernet
Honors IEEE 802.1p and DSCP priority tags
Jumbo frame: up to 9,720 bytes
Under the heading of "standards compliance" the vendor has provided a laundry list of the standards for which this switch can claim compliance. The first three items mean that the switch ports support twisted-pair Ethernet standards for 10/100/1000 Mbps speeds. These speeds are automatically selected while interacting with the client connection, using the Ethernet Auto-Negotiation protocol. Next, the vendor states that this switch will honor *Class of Service* priority tags on an Ethernet frame, by discarding traffic with lower-priority tags first in the event of port congestion. The last item in this laundry list notes that the switch can handle non-standard Ethernet frame sizes, often called "jumbo frames," which are sometimes configured on the Ethernet interfaces for a specific group of clients and their server(s) in an attempt to improve performance.[15]

This set of vendor specifications shows you what port speeds the switch supports and gives you an idea of how well the switch will perform in your system. When buying

---

15. Jumbo frames can be made to work locally for a specific set of machines that you manage and configure. However, the Internet consists of billions of Ethernet ports, all operating with the standard maximum frame size of 1,500 bytes. If you want things to work well over the Internet, stick with standard frame sizes.

larger and higher-performance switches intended for use in the core of a network, there are other switch specifications that you should consider. These include support for extra features like multicast management protocols, command line access to allow you to configure the switch, and the Simple Network Management Protocol to enable you to monitor the switch's operation and performance.

When using switches, you need to keep your network traffic requirements in mind. For example, if your network includes high-performance clients that place demands on a single server or set of servers, then whatever switch you use must have enough internal switching performance, high enough port speeds and uplink speeds, and sufficient port buffers to handle the task. In general, the higher-cost switches with high-performance switching fabrics also have good buffering levels, but you need to read the specifications carefully and compare different vendors to ensure that you are getting the best switch for the job.

CHAPTER 2

Basic Switch Features

Now that we've seen how switches function, we will describe some of the features you may find supported on switches. The size of your network and its expected growth affect the way you use Ethernet switches and the type of switch features that you need. A network in a home or single office space can get by with one or a few small and low-cost switches that provide basic Ethernet service at high enough speeds to meet your needs with few extra features. Such networks are not expected to be complex enough to present major challenges in terms of network stability, nor are they expected to grow much larger.

On the other hand, a medium-sized network supporting multiple offices may need more powerful switches with some management features and configuration capabilities. If the offices require high-performance networking for access to file servers, then the network design may require switches with fast uplink ports. Large campus networks with hundreds or even thousands of network connections will typically have a hier-archical network design based on switches with high-speed uplink ports, and more sophisticated switch features to support network management and help maintain net-work stability.

Switch Management

Depending on their cost, switches may be provided with a management interface and management software that collects and displays statistics on switch operation, network activity, and port traffic and error counters. Many medium- and higher-cost switches include some level of management capability, and vendors typically provide manage-ment application software that is Web-based and may also allow you to login to the switch via a console port on the switch or over the network.

The management software allows you to configure port speeds and features on the switch; it also provides monitoring information on switch operations and performance.

Switches that support the spanning tree protocol typically also support a management interface that allows you to configure spanning tree operations on each switch port. Other configurable options may include port speed, Ethernet auto-negotiation features, and any advanced switch features that may be supported.

Simple Network Management Protocol

Many switch management systems also use the *Simple Network Management Protocol (SNMP)* to provide a vendor-neutral way to extract operational information from a switch and deliver that data to you. That information typically includes the traffic rates being seen on switch ports, error counters that can identify devices that are having problems, and much more. Network management packages based on SNMP protocols can retrieve information from a wider range of network equipment than just switches.

There are multiple software packages available in the marketplace that can retrieve SNMP-based management information from the switch and display it to the network manager. There are also a number of open source packages that provide access to SNMP information and display that information in graphs and textual displays. See Appendix A for links to further information.

Packet Mirror Ports

Another useful feature for monitoring and troubleshooting switches is called a *packet mirror port*. This feature allows you to copy, or "mirror," the traffic from one or more ports on the switch to the mirror port. A laptop running a network analyzer application can be connected to the mirror port to provide network traffic analysis.

A mirror port can be a very useful feature that makes it possible for you to track down a network problem on devices connected to a given switch. Vendors have adopted a wide range of approaches to mirror ports, with different capabilities and limitations depending on their particular implementation. Some vendors even make it possible for mirrored traffic to be sent to a remote receiver over the network, which enables remote troubleshooting. Packet mirroring ports are not a standardized feature of switches, so vendors may or may not include this capability.

Switch Traffic Filters

Switch traffic filters make it possible for a network manager to specify Ethernet frame filtering based on a number of parameters. The range of filters supported by switches varies widely among vendors. Lower-cost devices with no management interface won't have any filtering capability, while higher-cost and higher-performance devices may offer a complete set of filters that the network manager can set.

By using these filters, a network manager can configure switches to control such things as network traffic based on the addresses of Ethernet frames, and the type of high-level protocol being carried in the frame. Filters may result in reduced performance, so you should check the switch documentation to determine the impact.

Filters work by comparing filter patterns, expressed as numeric values or protocol port names (e.g., http, ssh), against the bit patterns seen in Ethernet frames. When the pattern matches, then the filter takes some action, typically dropping the frame and thereby blocking the traffic.

 Be aware that by using filters, you may cause as many problems as you are trying to resolve.

Filters that are designed to match patterns in the data field of the frame can cause issues when those patterns also occur in frames that you did not want to filter. A filter set up to match on one set of hex digits at a given location in the data field of a frame may work fine for the network protocol you are trying to control, but could also block a network protocol you didn't even know existed.

This kind of filter is typically deployed to control the flow of some network protocol by identifying a part of the protocol in the data field of the Ethernet frame. Unfortunately, it's hard for a network manager to anticipate the range of data that the network may carry, and depending on how it was constructed, the filter may match frames that were not intended to be filtered. Debugging a failure caused by a wayward filter can be difficult, since it's usually not very obvious why an otherwise normally functioning Ethernet stops working for a specific application or for a certain set of stations.

Switch filters are often used in an attempt to gain greater control by preventing network interaction at the high-level network protocol layer of operations. If that's why you're implementing switch filters, then you should consider using Layer 3 routers that operate at the network layer and automatically provide this level of isolation without having to use manually-configured filters.

Layer 3 routers also provide filtering capabilities that can be easier to deploy since they are designed to work on high-level protocol fields and addresses. This makes it possible to easily write a filter that protects your network equipment from attack, for example, by limiting access to the TCP/IP management addresses of the equipment.

Managing switch filters

It can be a complex undertaking to set up filters correctly, as well as to maintain them once they are in place. As your network grows, you will need to keep track of which switches have filters in them, and to make sure that you can remember how the filters you have configured affect the operation of the network system, as it can often be difficult to predict the effect of a filter.

Documentation of the filters you have deployed and the way they are being used can help reduce troubleshooting time. However, no matter how well documented, these kinds of filters can cause outages. Therefore, you should regard the use of filters as something to be done only when necessary, and as carefully as possible.

Virtual LANs

A widely used feature typically included in higher-cost switches is the ability to group ports in a switch into virtual local area networks, or VLANs. At its simplest, a VLAN is a group of switch ports that function as though they are an independent switch. This is done by manipulating the frame forwarding software in the switch.

If the vendor supports VLANs on a switch, then they will provide a management interface to allow the network manager to configure which ports belong to which VLANs. As shown in Figure 2-1, we could configure an 8-port switch so that ports 1 through 4 are in one VLAN (call it VLAN 100), and ports 5 through 8 are in another VLAN (call it VLAN 200). Packets can be sent from station 10 to station 20, but not from station 10 to stations 30 and 40. Because these VLANs act as separate networks, a broadcast or multicast sent on VLAN 100 will not be transmitted on any ports belonging to VLAN 200. Therefore, the VLANs behave as though you had split the 8-port switch into two independent 4-port switches.

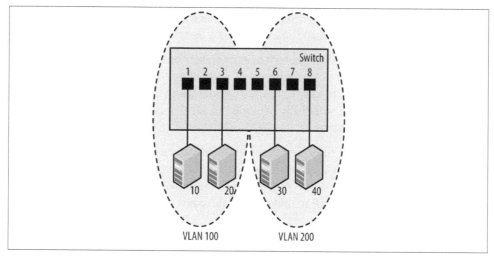

Figure 2-1. VLANs and switch ports

Vendors have provided other VLAN capabilities. For example, VLAN membership can be based on the contents of frames instead of just specifying which ports on the switch are members of a given VLAN. In this mode of operation, frames are passed through a set of filters as they are received on a switch port. The filters are set up to match some criterion, such as the source address in the frame or the contents of the type field, which specifies the high-level protocol carried in the data field of the frame. VLANs are defined based on their correspondence with these filters; depending on which set of criteria the frames match, the frames are automatically placed into the corresponding VLAN.

802.1Q VLAN Standard

The IEEE 802.1Q VLAN tagging standard was first published in 1998. This standard provides a vendor-independent way of implementing VLANs. The VLAN tagging scheme used in 802.1Q adds 4 bytes of information to the Ethernet frame, following the destination address and preceding the type/length field. This increases the maximum frame size in Ethernet to 1522 bytes, as shown in Figure 2-2.

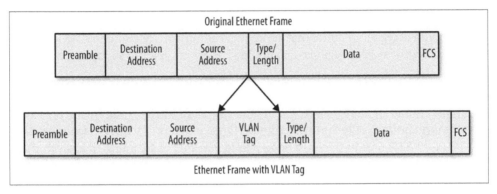

Figure 2-2. Ethernet frame with a VLAN tag

The 802.1Q standard also provides for priority handling of Ethernet frames using Class of Service (CoS) bits defined in the 802.1p standard. The 802.1Q standard provides space in the VLAN tag which allows you to use 802.1p CoS bits to indicate traffic priorities. There are three bits reserved for CoS values, making it possible to provide eight values (0-7) to identify frames with varying service levels.

Linking VLANs

VLANs are widely used in network designs to provide multiple independent networks. This helps control the flow of traffic by isolating traffic sent among specific groups of stations. Each VLAN functions as a separate switch, and there is no way to link separate VLANs other than connecting them together with a Layer 3 router. Building larger networks by linking VLANs with Layer 3 routers also avoids the propagation of broadcasts and multicasts seen on large Layer 2 networks, as it shifts the packet forwarding operations between the VLANs to a Layer 3 protocol.

802.1Q Multiple Spanning Tree Protocol

Multiple Spanning Tree Protocol (MSTP) was developed in the 802.1s supplement to the 802.1Q standard. It is defined as an optional extension to RSTP to add the ability for switches supporting VLANs to use multiple spanning trees. This makes it possible for traffic belonging to different VLANs to flow over different paths within the network. The operation of the MST standard was designed to minimize the number of BPDUs required to build spanning trees for multiple VLANs, and to therefore be a more efficient system.

Note that if there is only one VLAN in use, then either the classic spanning tree or the more recent rapid spanning tree protocols are sufficient. Even when there is more than one VLAN, classic and rapid spanning tree will still be able to block loop paths. The multiple spanning tree protocol provides a more efficient model of operation based on multiple spanning tree (MST) "regions" that can each run multiple MST instances. The inclusion of regions requires that the network administrator configure MST bridges to be members of specific regions, making MST more complex to set up and operate.

While the MST standard provides advantages in terms of structuring a large system into regions, it also requires more effort up front in order to understand the configuration requirements and to implement them in your switches. MSTP is optionally provided on some switches, typically those that support large numbers of VLANs. However, classic STP and RSTP remain the most widely-used versions of spanning tree, given their "plug and play" operation and their ability to create an effective spanning tree for the vast majority of network designs.

Quality of Service (QoS)

Managing the priority of traffic flow to favor certain categories of traffic over other categories when congestion occurs is another capability of switches. The 32-bit field added by the IEEE 802.1Q standard provides support for traffic prioritization fields to utilize eight different Class of Service values as well as the VLAN tag.

The 802.1p standard provides traffic prioritization levels that are carried in the 802.1Q CoS tag and used to tag a frame with a priority value, so that certain traffic may be favored for transmission when network congestion occurs on a switch port. When CoS has been configured on a switch port, then the Ethernet frames that are not tagged with a high priority are the first to be dropped, should congestion occur on the port.

If your switch supports these features, you will need to consult the vendor documentation for instructions on how to configure them. While the IEEE standards describe the mechanisms that make these features possible, the standards do not specify how they should be implemented or configured. That's left up to each vendor to decide, which means that the vendor documentation is the place to find the details on how to use these features in a given switch.

CHAPTER 3

Network Design with Ethernet Switches

In this chapter, we will show some of the basic ways switches can be used to build an Ethernet system. Network design is a large topic, and there are many ways to use switches to expand and improve networks. We will focus on just a few basic designs here, with the goal of providing a brief introduction to network design using Ethernet switches.

Advantages of Switches in Network Designs

Switches provide multiple advantages in network designs. To begin with, all switches provide the basic traffic filtering functions described earlier, which improves network bandwidth. Another important advantage of modern switches is that the internal switching circuits allow traffic flows to simultaneously occur between multiple ports. Supporting multiple simultaneous flows of traffic, or "conversations," between the ports is a major advantage of switches in network designs.

Improved Network Performance

An important way in which a switch can improve the operation of a network system is by controlling the flow of traffic. The ability to intelligently forward traffic on only those ports needed to get the packet to its destination makes the switch a useful tool for the Ethernet designer faced with continually growing device populations and increasing traffic loads.

The traffic control provided by the internal address database can be exploited to help isolate traffic. By locating client and server connections on switches to help minimize network traffic, you can keep the traffic between a set of clients and their file server localized to the ports on a single switch. This keeps their traffic from having to traverse the larger network system.

Figure 3-1 shows a set of clients and their file server connected to a single switch, Switch 2, which isolates their traffic from the rest of the network connections in the building. In this design, all of the local traffic among clients 40, 50 and 60 and their file server stays on Switch 2 and does not travel through any other switches in the building.

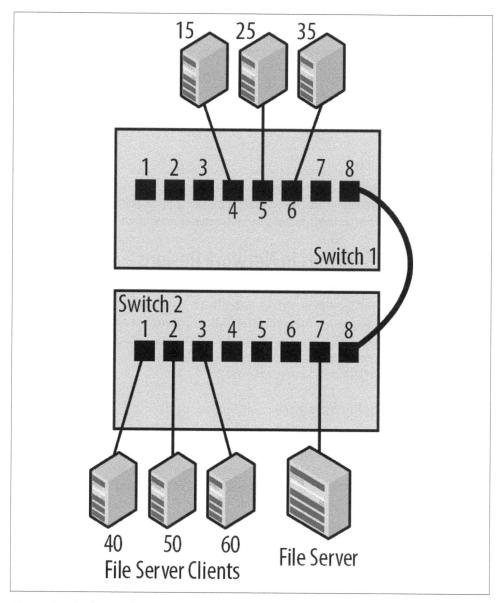

Figure 3-1. Isolating client-server traffic

When installing a switch, you can improve your network's operation by being aware of the traffic flows and designing the network so that the traffic between a cluster of clients and their server(s) stays local. You may not be able to do this for all clients in a building, but any clients and servers that you can keep on a single switch, or small group of switches, will help minimize the amount of traffic that has to cross all switches in your network.

The example in Figure 3-1 reveals another important issue, which is that the links used to connect switches together should be high-performance links. Links between switches are called *uplinks*, since network tree diagrams are typically drawn with the switches arranged in a top-to-bottom hierarchy. The top-most switch is the core switch, which functions as the core of the network system by linking all other switches.

Linking the *edge* switches directly to the core in this fashion minimizes the number of switches, or *switch hops*, that the network traffic must cross to get from one computer to another in your network. Uplinks connect one switch to the next, leading up to a higher level of the network (core). Traffic travels in both directions over the uplinks.

Switch Hierarchy and Uplink Speeds

Another advantage of switches is that they can link multiple network connections that run at different speeds. Any given connection to a switch port runs at a single speed, but multiple computers can be connected to the same switch, with the connections operating at different speeds. Depending on its cost and feature set, you may find that your switch has a couple of ports that are described as uplink ports. These ports typically support higher speeds than the rest of the ports on the switch, and are intended for making a connection up to the core switches, hence the term "uplink."

If you want to use the latest network jargon, you could say that the uplink ports are used to create "northbound" connections to the core of your network.

Switch ports can run at different speeds because a switch is equipped with multiple Ethernet interfaces, each capable of operating at any of the speeds supported on the interface. A switch can receive an Ethernet frame on a port operating at 1 Gb/s, store the frame in port buffer memory, and then transmit the frame on a port operating at 10 Gb/s.

Filling the port buffer and causing congestion and dropped frames is more likely to occur when receiving on a 10 Gb/s port and sending on a 1 Gb/s port. This is due to the large difference in speeds and the longer time it takes to send a frame out the 1 Gb/s port.

In Figure 3-2, three edge switches are shown, each with one of their uplink ports connected to a fourth switch located at the core of the network. While the uplink ports operate at 10 Gb/s, most of the station connections are at 1 Gb/s except for the file server, which is connected to a 10 Gb/s port.

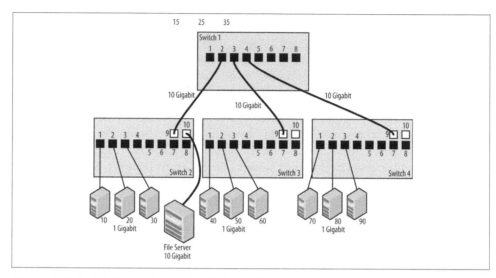

Figure 3-2. Switch hierarchy and uplink speeds

This connection shows that it's possible to connect the server to one of the uplink ports, since there's nothing that prohibits an uplink port from operating as a station port. Uplink ports typically operate at higher speeds, with larger packet buffers to handle traffic that arrives at higher speeds on the uplink port (10 Gb/s) and is destined for a slower station port (1 Gb/s). For that reason, while you usually want to save these ports for uplink purposes, they can also be used to connect to a heavily-used server machine.

Uplink Speeds and Traffic Congestion

The main reason you want uplinks to run faster is that there may be traffic from multiple stations connected at 1 Gb/s attempting to get to a single server on a separate switch. If the uplink connections were also running at 1 Gb/s, then there could be congestion and dropped frames, which can cause reduced performance for the computers sending data.

The port buffers on a switch are designed to hold just a few packets for a short period, which allows for a small amount of congestion. If the buffers were too large there could be increased packet delay and variation in packet delivery times, causing problems for certain kinds of applications. If there is a lot of traffic continually being sent from clients into one or more congested ports, the switch will run out of space in the port buffer memory, and will simply drop the incoming packets until space becomes available.

Local area networks are not designed to provide guaranteed packet delivery. If the system becomes congested, packets are dropped. The TCP/IP network protocol, in turn, is designed to respond to dropped frames by automatically throttling the traffic rate. In other words, dropped frames are normal and in fact are required to allow TCP/IP to detect and respond to network congestion.

To see how this works, let's take the example shown in Figure 3-2. Suppose that the three stations, 70, 80, and 90 on Switch 4, all need to retrieve files from the file server on Switch 2. File service traffic tends to be high bandwidth; you could easily end up with three 1 Gb/s streams from the file server to the stations on Switch 4. If the uplink connections are operating at 1 Gb/s, then the switch ports in the path between the stations on Switch 4 and the file server on Switch 2 will become congested and will drop the frames that cannot fit into the already-full port buffers.

If, on the other hand, you link the switches together with 10 Gb/s uplinks, then you have a 10 Gb/s path from the file server on Switch 2 into Switch 4, and all three stations on Switch 4 will be able to interact with the file server at their maximum network rate of 1 Gb/s, without causing major congestion on the uplink paths. Packets received at 1 Gb/s from the stations will be sent ten times as fast, at 10 Gb/s, over the uplinks; this rapidly drains the uplink port buffers and ensures that there is buffer space available for more traffic from other stations.

Another possible design is to connect the server directly to the core switch on a 10Gb/s port.

Multiple Conversations

The connection method shown here for the uplinks illustrates a couple of major advantages of switches: the ability to provide large amounts of packet switching performance inside the switch and the capacity to support multiple simultaneous traffic flows between stations and the file server. Every port on the switch in our example is an independent network connection, and each station gets its own 1 Gb/s dedicated full-duplex Ethernet path directly into the switch. Multiple station conversations occur simultaneously in both directions (data from the computer and replies to the computer), providing high performance and minimizing network delay.

Referring back to Figure 3-2, this means that while station 70 and the file server are communicating, station 80 and station 10 can be communicating at the same time. In this configuration, the total network bandwidth available to stations becomes a function of the ports to which each station is connected, and of the total packet switching capacity of your switch. Modern switches are equipped with switching fabrics that can provide many gigabits per second of switching capacity, and high-end switches will provide up to several terabits of packet switching capacity.

The speed of the switching fabric is only one important consideration when it comes to moving frames through a switch. As we've seen, high traffic rates coming into the switch from multiple ports, all destined for a single server port on the switch, will always be an issue, since the server port can only deliver packets at its maximum bit rate, no matter how many packets are sent to it at any given moment.

Switch Traffic Bottlenecks

When multiple flows occur, it's possible to overrun the capability of the output port, no matter how much internal packet switching capacity the switch may have. The switch will start dropping frames when it runs out of buffer space to store them temporarily. A dropped frame causes the network protocol software running on the computer to detect the loss and retransmit the data. Too many data retransmissions caused by excessive congestion on an output port can lead to a slow response for the application that is trying to talk to the server.

Traffic bottlenecks such as these are an issue in all network designs. When linking switches together, you may encounter situations where a bottleneck occurs when all the traffic from multiple switches must travel over single backbone links connecting two core switches. If there are multiple parallel connections linking the core switches, the spanning tree algorithm will ensure that only one path is active, in order to prevent loops in the network. Therefore, the ports of the switches that feed the single inter-core-switch link could be facing the same situation as the oversubscribed server port mentioned previously, causing the core switch ports to drop frames. In sufficiently large and busy network systems, a single inter-switch link may not provide enough bandwidth, leading to congestion.

There are several approaches that can be taken to avoid these problems in network systems. For example, the IEEE 802.1AX *Link Aggregation* standard allows multiple parallel Ethernet links to be grouped together and used as a large "virtual" channel between backbone switches.[1] Using link aggregation, multiple *Gigabit Ethernet* links can be aggregated into channels operating at two, four, and eight gigabits per second. The same is true for 10-Gigabit links, providing a channel operating up to 80 gigabits per second. This approach can also be used between a switch and Ethernet interfaces in high-performance servers to increase network bandwidth.

---

1. Link aggregation was first defined in the IEEE 802.3ad standard, and then later moved to become 802.1AX. You will find both standards referred to in vendor documentation.

Another approach is to use Layer 3 routers instead of Layer 2 switches, since routers don't use the spanning tree algorithm. Instead, routers provide more sophisticated traffic routing mechanisms that make it possible for network designers to provide multiple parallel connections for backbone links that are simultaneously active.

Hierarchical Network Design

Network design refers to the way that switches are interconnected to produce a larger network system. Any network with more than just a few switches, and especially any network that is expected to grow, will benefit from a hierarchical network design that results in a system that is higher performance, more reliable, and easier to troubleshoot. Implementing a network design, and thus providing a plan for optimizing network operation and growth, pays major dividends in terms of network performance and reliability.

Networks that grow without a plan often result in systems with switches connected together in such a way that there are more switches in the traffic paths than necessary. This, in turn, leads to more complex "mesh" designs that are harder to understand and troubleshoot. Another name for the result of network growth with no plan is "fur ball" design. (Or perhaps it should be called "hair ball.") Systems that "just grew" may also develop traffic bottlenecks whose presence and location are mysterious to the network administrator.

It's a fact of life that networks often grow; without an adequate design in place they will grow randomly, becoming ever more complex and difficult to understand. A simple hierarchical network design based on two or three "layers" minimizes the number of switches needed, improving traffic flow and resulting in improved network performance and reliability. Other important advantages are that the network will be more stable and understandable as the system grows over time.

The most widely deployed design for networks that support standard offices and cube space in a campus of buildings is based on a hierarchical system of three layers: Core, Distribution, and Access, as shown in Figure 3-3. The core layer contains the high-performance switches that connect all buildings on a campus together. Each building has a distribution point, which contains the medium-performance switches connecting the building to the core and also connecting to the access switches inside the building. Finally, there is an access layer comprised of switches, which connects to all devices in the building; the access layer switches are connected in turn to the distribution switches. If there is only a single building, then the distribution and access layers are the only ones needed, with the distribution layer functioning as the building core.

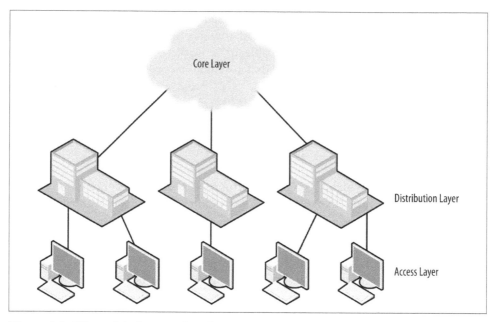

Figure 3-3. Hierarchical network architecture

Inside each building, the access switches are connected directly to the distribution layer, and *not* to each other, as shown in Figure 3-4 It is essential that the uplinks of the access switches are connected only to the distribution layer switches, in order to avoid creating a set of horizontal paths between the access switches with a much more complex mesh structure. A major benefit of this design is that it reduces the number of switches in the network path between communicating Ethernet devices. That, in turn, decreases the impact of switch latency, and also reduces the number of bottlenecks affecting network traffic.

This design also minimizes the number of potential loop paths, which helps the spanning tree protocol converge on a set of paths more rapidly. This can become especially important after a power failure in a complex network, when all switches come back up at the same time and spanning tree must work to stabilize the entire set of network paths simultaneously. A hierarchical network design also makes it easier to provide high bandwidth uplinks, which helps prevent major bottlenecks and keeps spanning tree working well under all network load conditions.

Establishing and maintaining a network design requires documentation and attention to detail. Everyone involved in maintaining the network needs to understand the design in use and the benefits of maintaining a good network structure. You will find further reading on network design in the Appendix A.

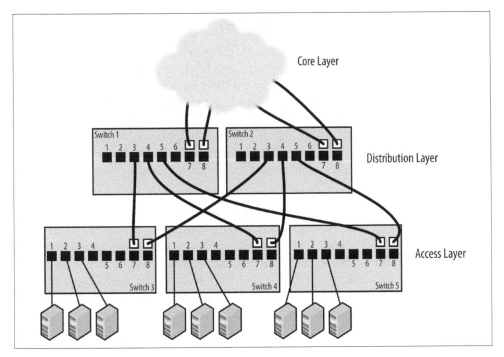

Figure 3-4. Distribution network in a building

Seven Hop Maximum

As we've just seen, there are multiple reasons for minimizing the number of switches in the network path between devices. The 802.1D bridging standard provided yet another reason when it recommended a maximum network diameter of seven hops, meaning seven switches in the path between any two stations.

The recommended limit on the number of switches originated in a concern about round-trip packet delays with seven switches in a given path, providing 14 switch hops in a total round trip. A time-sensitive application sending a frame from one end of the network to the other and receiving a reply would encounter 14 switch hops, with the potential for an impact on the performance of the application, because of the time required to transit 14 switches.

The seven hop recommendation was in all versions of the 802.1D standard up to 1998. Subsequent versions of the standard removed the seven hop recommendation from the standard. However, in large network designs your network design should serve to keep the total number of switch hops to a minimum.

Network Resiliency with Switches

Network systems support access to the Internet and to all manner of local computing resources, making them essential to everyone's productivity. If the network fails, it will have a major impact on everyone's ability to get their work done. Fortunately, network equipment tends to be highly reliable, and equipment failures are rare. Having said that, network equipment is just another computer in a box. There are no perfect machines; at some point you *will* have a switch failure. The power supply may quit working, causing the entire switch to fail, or one or more ports may fail. If an uplink port fails, it could isolate an entire downstream switch, cutting off network access for every station connected to that switch.

One way to avoid network outages due to a switch failure is to build resilient networks based on the use of multiple switches. You could purchase two core switches, call them Switch 1 and Switch 2, and connect them together over parallel paths, so that there are two links between them in case one of the links fails. Next, you could link each of the access switches that connect to stations to both core switches. In other words, on each access layer switch, one of the two uplink ports is connected to core Switch 1 and the other uplink port is connected to core Switch 2.

Figure 3-5 shows the two core switches, Switch 1 and Switch 2, connected together over two parallel paths to provide a resilient connection in case one of the links fails for any reason. The aggregation switches are each connected to both core switches, providing two paths to the network core in case any single path fails.

Spanning Tree and Network Resiliency

At this point you should be asking, "But what about spanning tree? Won't it shut down those parallel paths between resilient switches?" The answer is yes, spanning tree will block one of the two paths to ensure that there are no loop paths in the network system. The path will stay blocked until one of the active links fails, in which case RTSP, responding quickly to a detected change in the network, will immediately bring the backup paths into operation.

Figure 3-6 shows the resilient design after spanning tree has suppressed the loop paths by blocking the forwarding of packets on certain uplink ports. The ports that are blocked are shown with a "B." If you know the MAC addresses and bridge IDs for each switch, then you can calculate, based on the operation of the spanning tree protocol, exactly which ports will be blocked to prevent loop paths.

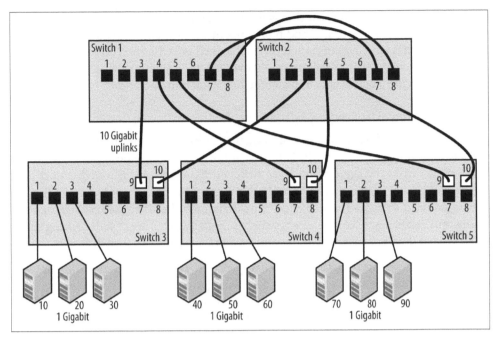

Figure 3-5. Network resiliency with switches

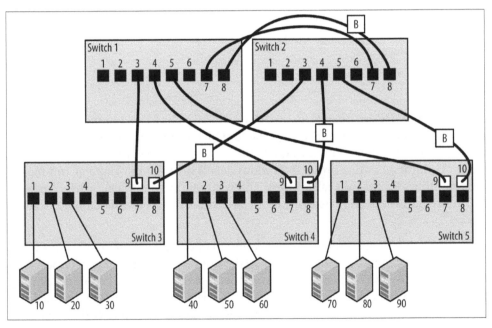

Figure 3-6. Spanning tree suppresses loop paths

But you don't need to know how things work at that level of detail. Instead, spanning tree will function automatically, and block one of the two paths creating a loop. The Ethernet link stays up and connected on the blocked port, but no traffic is forwarded over it. If the remaining active path should ever fail, then spanning tree will automatically re-enable the blocked port to bring the link back into operation.

Cost and complexity of resiliency

The combination of dual core switches, dual uplinks, and spanning tree provides a resilient design that can survive the failure of one of the core switches and/or one of the dual uplinks from the aggregation layer switches. However, this is a higher cost and higher complexity design that requires both a larger budget and an understanding of how to connect switches for resilience. This design also has the disadvantage of providing only resiliency. All of the access switch links to Switch 2 are in the blocking state, and Switch 2 does not carry any traffic unless there is a failure of Switch 1.

If your network uptime needs are not so stringent as to require the kind of high uptime and automatic failure recovery provided by this design, then you could get by with keeping a spare switch on hand and using it to replace failures when they occur. It's all a matter of your tolerance for network downtime and how much you are willing to invest in avoiding outages with automatic recovery systems.

Network design issues such as these require a good deal of knowledge about the mechanisms used to direct the flow of traffic through various devices such as switches and routers. This is also an area that is undergoing rapid evolution, and new mechanisms for moving traffic around large networks are continually being invented and tried out in the marketplace.

Routers

A router is a device that operates at the "Network" layer, or Layer 3 of the OSI network reference model. It helps to understand that the OSI layers are not derived from physics or the natural laws of the universe. Quite the opposite. Instead, the OSI layers are arbitrary definitions used to group the various details involved in computer communications into associated tasks called layers. This was done as a way to help clarify the tasks and to structure the development of the standards needed to achieve the communication tasks.

Like many other human endeavors, the evolution of computer communications technology has not followed a completely logical development path. For example, local area networks were defined as operating at Layer 2 because that's what the people developing the standards wanted: a local network that carried data between computers located at a given site. Layer 2 standards describe local area networks operating at the Data Link

Layer, and were not intended to deal with the issues of interconnecting large numbers of networks.

More sophisticated protocol operations based on structured addresses and capable of dealing with large numbers of networks were defined at Layer 3, the Network Layer. Switches operate at Layer 2 using only the information found in Ethernet frames, and routers operate at Layer 3 using high level network protocol packets carried in the data field of Ethernet frames, such as those packets defined in the TCP/IP protocol suite. Both Layer 2 and Layer 3 switches use Ethernet frames, but the addressing information used by the switch to make a packet forwarding decision is very different.

Operation and Use of Routers

Routers are frequently used in large campus and enterprise networks, as well as the Internet itself. At the network layer of operation, you can find a wider range of mechanisms for interconnecting large network systems. While routers are more complex to configure than switches, the advantages they can provide offset the added complexity of their operation for many network managers.

In operation, a router receives and unpacks the Ethernet frames, and then applies rules to deal appropriately with the high-level protocol data that is carried in the data field of each Ethernet frame. When a router hears an Ethernet broadcast, it does the same thing all other stations must do: it reads the frame in and tries to figure out what to do with it.

Since routers move packets around based on higher-level protocol addresses, they do not forward Ethernet broadcast or multicast packets. Broadcast or multicast packets sent from a client station attempting to discover a service on a server connected to the same local network, for example, are not forwarded to other networks by the router, because the router is not designed to create a larger local area network.

Dropping broadcasts and multicasts at the router interface creates separate broadcast domains, protecting a large network system from the high multicast and broadcast traffic rates that might otherwise occur. This is a major advantage, both as a result of the reduced traffic levels, and the reduction in computer performance issues that can be caused by floods of broadcast and multicast packets.

Dividing networks into multiple, smaller Layer 2 networks by linking them with Layer 3 routers also improves reliability by limiting the size of the *failure domain*. In the event of such failures as packet floods caused by loop paths, a failing station that is sending continuous broadcast or multicast traffic, or hardware or software failure resulting in a failure of spanning tree, the size of the failure domain is limited by using Layer 3 routers to link networks.

However, creating smaller Layer 2 networks and linking them with Layer 3 routers also limits the number of stations that can interact when using discovery services based on

Layer 2 multicast and broadcast. That, in turn, may cause challenges for network designers who are attempting to grow their network and limit the size of their failure domains while also keeping their users happy.

Users are happiest when everything "just works," and are often insistent on large Layer 2 networks to keep automatic service discovery working for the largest number of computers. However, when a large Layer 2 network fails, users may suddenly discover that network reliability based on smaller networks connected with Layer 3 routers is more important to them than the convenience of widespread Layer 2 service discovery. See Appendix A for more information on network design issues.

Routers or Bridges?

Although both Layer 2 switches (bridges) and Layer 3 switches (routers) can be used to extend Ethernets by building larger network systems, bridges and routers operate in very different ways. It's up to you to decide which device is best suited to your needs, and which set of capabilities is most important for your network design. Both bridges and routers have advantages and disadvantages.

Advantages of bridges

- Bridges may provide larger amounts of switching bandwidth and more ports at lower cost than a router.
- Bridges may operate faster than a router, since they provide fewer functions.
- Bridges are typically simpler to install and operate.
- Bridges are transparent to the operation of an Ethernet.
- Bridges provide automatic network traffic isolation (except for broadcasts and multicasts).

Disadvantages of bridges

- Bridges propagate multicast and broadcast frames. This allows broadcasts to travel throughout your network, making stations vulnerable to floods of broadcast traffic that may be generated by network software bugs, poorly designed software, or inadvertent network loops on a switch that doesn't support the spanning tree protocol.
- Bridges typically cannot load-share across multiple network paths. However, you may be able to use the link aggregation protocol to provide load sharing capabilities across multiple aggregated links.

Advantages of routers

- Routers automatically direct traffic to specific portions of the network based on the Internet Protocol (IP) destination address, providing better traffic control.
- Routers block the flow of broadcasts and multicasts. Routers also structure the flow of traffic throughout a network system based on Layer 3 network protocol addresses. This allows you to design more complex network topologies, while still retaining high stability for network operations as your network system grows and evolves.
- Routers use routing protocols that can provide information such as the bandwidth of a path. Using that information, routers can provide best-path routing and use multiple paths to provide load sharing.
- Routers provide greater network manageability in terms of access control filters and restricting access based on IP addresses.

Disadvantages of routers

- Router operation is not automatic, making routers more complex to configure.
- Routers may be more expensive and may provide fewer ports than switches do.

The state of the art for bridges and routers is constantly evolving, and today many high-end switches are capable of operating as bridges and routers simultaneously, combining Layer 2 bridging and Layer 3 routing capabilities in the same device, as described in "Multilayer Switches" on page 45. You need to evaluate these approaches to establishing a network design and building a network system, given the requirements of your network.

CHAPTER 4

Special-Purpose Switches

Previously, we described basic switch operation and features. Ethernet switches are building blocks of modern networking, and switches are used to build every kind of network imaginable. To meet these needs, vendors have created a wide range of Ethernet switch types and switch features. In this chapter we cover several special-purpose switches, many developed for specific network types. The Ethernet switch market is a big place, and here we can only provide an overview of some of the different kinds of switches that are available.

We begin with a look at various kinds of switches sold for specific markets. There are switches designed for enterprise and campus networks, data center networks, Internet Service Provider networks, industrial networks, and more. Within each category there are also multiple switch models.

Multilayer Switches

As networks became more complex and switches evolved, the development of the multilayer switch combined the roles of bridging and routing in a single device. This made it possible to purchase a single switch that could perform both kinds of packet forwarding: bridging at Layer 2 and routing at Layer 3. Early bridges and routers were separate devices, each with a specific role to play in building networks. Ethernet switches typically provided high-performance bridging across a lot of ports, and routers specialized in providing high-level protocol forwarding (routing) across a smaller set of ports. By combining those functions, a multilayer switch could provide benefits to the network designer.

As you might expect, a multilayer switch is more complex to configure. However, by providing both bridging and routing in the same device, a multilayer switch makes it easier to build large and complex networks that combine the advantages of both forms of packet forwarding. This makes it possible for vendors to provide high-performance operation of both bridging and routing across a large set of Ethernet ports at a competitive price point.

Large, multilayer switches are often used in the core of a network system to provide both Layer 2 switching and Layer 3 routing, depending on requirements. As networks grow, Layer 3 routing can provide isolation between Ethernet systems and help enable a network plan based on a hierarchical design. Multilayer switches are also used as distribution switches in a building, providing an aggregation point for access switches. Layer 3 routing in an aggregation switch can provide separate Layer 3 networks per VLAN in a building, improving isolation, resiliency, and performance.

Access Switches

In a large enterprise network, the bulk of the network connections are on the edge, where access switches are used to connect to end nodes such as desktop computers. As a result, there is a large marketplace for access switches, with multiple vendors and a wide variety of features and price points.

When it comes to building large networks with dozens, or even hundreds or thousands of access switches, a major consideration is the set of features that can provide ease of monitoring and management. Other considerations may include whether the access switches support high speed uplinks, whether they include features like multicast packet management, and whether their internal switching speeds are capable of handling all ports running at maximum packet rates.

Each vendor has a story to tell about their access switch capabilities and how they can help make it easier for you to build and manage a network. While it's a significant task to compare and contrast the various access switches, you can learn a lot in the process and it will help you make an informed purchasing decision.

Stacking Switches

Some switches are designed to allow "stacking," or combining a set of switches to operate as a single switch. Stacking makes it possible to combine multiple switches that support 24 or 48 ports each, for example, and manage the stacked set of switches and switch ports as a single, logical switch that supports the combined set of ports. Stacking also provides benefits when replacing a failed switch that is a member of the stack, since the replacement switch can be automatically re-configured with the software and configuration from the failed switch, making it possible to quickly and easily restore network service.

Stacking switches are linked together with special cables to create the physical and logical stack, as shown in Figure 4-1. These cables are typically kept as short as possible, and the switches are placed directly on top of each other, forming a compact stack of equipment that functions as a single switch. There is no IEEE standard for stacking; each vendor offering this feature has their own stacking cables and connectors.

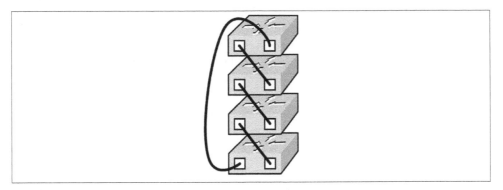

Figure 4-1. Stacking switches

The stacking cables create a backplane between the switches, but the packet switching speeds supported between switches in a stacking system vary, depending on the vendor. Some stacking switches are designed to use 10 Gigabit Ethernet cables connected between their uplink ports to create a stack. In this case, the stacking cable is a standard Ethernet patch cable, but the stacking software running on the switches is specific to the vendor. As a result, you cannot mix and match stacking switches from different vendors.

Industrial Ethernet

Industrial Ethernet switches are switches that have been "hardened" to make it possible for them to function in the harsh environments found in factories and other industrial settings. Industrial Ethernet switches are used to support industrial automation and control systems, as well as network connections to instrumentation for the control and monitoring of major infrastructures, such as the electrical power grid.

Industrial Ethernet switches may also feature special port connections that provide a seal around the Ethernet cable to keep moisture and dirt out of the switch ports. The switch itself may be sealed and fanless, to avoid exposing the internal electronics to a harsh environment. You may also find ratings for the G-forces and vibrations that industrial switches can handle. To make it possible to meet the stringent environmental specifications, industrial switches are often built as smaller units, with a limited set of ports.

Wireless Access Point Switches

The development of wireless Ethernet switches is a recent innovation. Wireless Ethernet is a marketing term for the IEEE 802.11 wireless LAN (WLAN) standard, which provides wireless data services, also known as "Wi-Fi." Wireless Ethernet vendors provide a wide range of approaches to building and running a WLAN, with one widely adopted approach consisting of access points connected to WLAN controllers. A wireless LAN controller provides support for the APs, helping to maintain the operation of the wireless system through such functions as automatic wireless channel assignment and radio power management. Typically, the controller is located in the core of a network, and wireless AP data flows are connected to the controller either directly over a VLAN, or via packet tunneling over a Layer 3 network system.

Wireless vendors have extended the controller approach by combining the controller software with a standard Ethernet switch. Including wireless controller functions and wired Ethernet ports in a single device reduces cost and makes it possible for the wireless system to grow larger without overloading a central controller. Wireless switches typically include ports equipped with Power over Ethernet, powering the APs and managing their data and operation in a single device.

A typical wireless user in an enterprise or corporate network is required to authenticate themselves before being allowed to access the wireless system, which improves security and makes it possible to manage the system down to the individual user. Wireless Ethernet switches can also provide client authentication services on wired ports, extending the wireless user management capabilities to the wired Ethernet system.

Internet Service Provider Switches

In recent years, Ethernet has made inroads in the Internet service provider marketplace, providing switches that are used by carriers to build wide area networks that span entire continents and the globe. ISPs have specialized requirements based on their need to provide multiple kinds of networking. ISPs provide high-speed and high-performance links over long distances, but they may also provide metro-area links between businesses in a given city, as well as links to individual users to provide Internet services at homes.

None of the ISP and carrier networks are particularly "local" in the sense of the original "local area network" design for Ethernet. The development of full-duplex Ethernet links freed Ethernet from the timing constraints of the old half-duplex media system, and made it possible to use Ethernet technology to make network connections over much longer distances than envisioned in the original LAN standard. With the local area network distance limitations eliminated, carriers and ISPs were then able to exploit the high volume Ethernet market to help lower their costs by providing Ethernet links for long distances, metro areas, and home networks.

Metro Ethernet

While the IEEE standardizes Ethernet technology and basic switch functions, there are sets of switch features that are used in the carrier and ISP marketplaces to meet the needs of those specific markets. To meet their requirements, businesses have formed forums and alliances to help identify the switch features that are most important to them, and to publish specifications that include specialized methods of configuring switches, which improve interoperability between equipment from different vendors.

One example of this is the Metro Ethernet Forum.[1] In January, 2013, the MEF announced the certifications for equipment that can be configured to meet "Carrier Ethernet 2.0" specifications. The set of CE 2.0 specifications include Ethernet switch features that provide a common platform for delivering services of use to carriers and ISPs. By carefully specifying these services, the MEF seeks to create a standard set of services and a network design that is distinguished from typical enterprise Ethernet systems by five "attributes." The attributes include services of interest to carriers and ISPs, along with specifications to help achieve scalability, reliability, quality of service, and service management.

The Metro Ethernet Forum is an example of a business alliance developing a comprehensive set of specifications that help define Ethernet switch operation for metro, carrier, and ISP networks. These specifications rely on a set of switch features, some of them quite complex, that are needed to achieve their network design goals, but which typically don't apply to an enterprise or campus network design.

Data Center Switches

Data center networks have a set of requirements that reflect the importance of data centers as sites that host hundreds or thousands of servers providing Internet and application services to clients. Corporate data centers hold critically important servers whose failure could affect the operations of major portions of the company, as well as the company's customers. Because of the intense network performance requirements caused by placing many critically important servers in the same room, data center networks use some of the most advanced Ethernet switches and switch features available.

---

1. The MEF (*http://bit.ly/meforum*) describes itself as: "… a global industry alliance comprising more than 200 organizations including telecommunications service providers, cable MSOs, network equipment/software manufacturers, semiconductors vendors and testing organizations. The MEF's mission is to accelerate the worldwide adoption of Carrier-class Ethernet networks and services. The MEF develops Carrier Ethernet technical specifications and implementation agreements to promote interoperability and deployment of Carrier Ethernet worldwide."

Data Center Port Speeds

Some data center servers provide database access or storage access used by other high-performance servers in the data center, requiring 10 Gb/s ports to avoid bottlenecks. Major servers providing public services, such as access to World Wide Web pages, may also need 10 Gb/s interfaces, depending on how many clients they must serve simultaneously.

Data center servers also host virtual machines (VMs) in which a single server will run software that functions as multiple, virtual servers. There can be many VMs per server, and hundreds or thousands of virtual machines per data center. As each VM is a separate operating system running separate services, the large number of VMs also increases the network traffic generated by each physical server.

Data center switches typically feature non-blocking internal packet switching fabrics, to avoid any internal switch bottlenecks. These switches also feature high speed ports, since modern servers are equipped with Gigabit Ethernet interfaces and many of them come with interfaces that can run at both 1 and 10 Gb/s.

Data Center Switch Types

Data centers consist of equipment cabinets or racks aligned in rows, with servers mounted in dense stacks, using mounting hardware that screws into flanges. When you open the door to one of these cabinets, you are faced with a tightly-packed stack of servers, one on top of the other, filling the cabinet space. One method for providing switch ports in a cabinet filled with servers is to locate a "top of rack," or TOR, switch at the top of the cabinet, and to connect the servers to ports on that switch.

The TOR switch connects, in turn, to larger and more powerful switches located either in the middle of a row, or in the end cabinet of a row. The row switches, in their turn, are connected to core switches located in a core row in the data center. This provides a "core, aggregation, edge" design. Each of the three types of switches has a different set of capabilities that reflect the role of the switch.

The TOR switch is designed to be as low cost as possible, as befits an edge switch that connects to all stations. However, data center networks require high performance, so the TOR switch must be able to handle the *throughput*. The row switches must also be high-performance, to allow them to aggregate the uplink connections from the TOR switches. Finally, the core switches must be very high-performance and provide enough high-speed uplink ports to connect to all row switches.

Data Center Oversubscription

Oversubscription is common in engineering, and describes a system which is provisioned to meet the typical demand on the system rather than the absolute maximum demand. This reduces expense and avoids purchasing resources that would rarely, or never, be used. In network designs, oversubscription makes it possible to avoid purchasing excess switch and port performance.

When you're dealing with the hundreds and thousands of high-performance ports that may be present in a modern data center, it can be quite difficult to provide enough bandwidth for the entire network to be "non-blocking," meaning that all ports can simultaneously operate at their maximum performance. Rather than provide a non-blocking system, a network that is oversubscribed can serve all users economically, without a significant impact on their performance.

As an example, a non-blocking network design for one hundred 10 Gb/s ports located on a single row of a data center would have to provide 1 terabit of bandwidth to the core switches. If all 8 rows of a data center each needed to support one hundred 10 Gb/s ports, that would require 8 terabits of port speed up to the core, and an equivalent amount of switching capability in the core switches. Providing that kind of performance is very expensive.

But, even if you had the money and space to provide that many high-performance switches and ports, the large investment in network performance would be wasted, since the bandwidth would be mostly unused. Although a given server or set of servers may be high-performance, in the vast majority of data centers not all servers are running at maximum performance all of the time. In most network systems, the Ethernet links tend to run at low average bit rates, interspersed with higher rate bursts of traffic. Thus, you do not need to provide 100 percent simultaneous throughput for all ports in the majority of network designs, including most data centers. Instead, typical data center designs can include a significant level of oversubscription without affecting performance in any significant way.

Data Center Switch Fabrics

Data centers continue to grow, and server connection speeds continue to increase, placing more pressure on data center networks to handle large amounts of traffic without excessive costs. To meet these needs, vendors are developing new switch designs, generally called "data center switch fabrics." These fabrics combine switches in ways that increase performance and reduce oversubscription.

Each of the major vendors has a different approach to the problem, and there is no one definition for a data center fabric. There are both vendor proprietary approaches and standards-based approaches that are called "Ethernet fabrics," and it is up to the marketplace to decide which approach or set of approaches will be widely adopted. Data center networks are evolving rapidly, and network designers must work especially hard to understand the options and their capabilities and costs.

Data Center Switch Resiliency

A major goal of data centers is high availability, since any failure of access can affect large numbers of people. To achieve that goal, data centers implement resilient network designs based on the use of multiple switches supporting multiple connections to servers. As with other areas of network design, resilient approaches are evolving through the efforts of multiple vendors and the development of new standards.

One way to achieve resiliency for server connections in a data center is to provide two switches in a given row—call them Switch A and Switch B—and connect the server to both switches. To exploit this resiliency, some vendors provide "multi-chassis link aggregation" (MLAG), in which software running on both switches makes the switches appear as to the server to be a single switch.

The server thinks that it is connected to two Ethernet links on a single switch using standard 802.1AX link aggregation (LAG) protocols. But in reality, there are two switches involved in providing the aggregated link. Should a port or an entire switch fail for any reason, the server still has an active connection to the data center network and will not be isolated from the network. Note that MLAG is currently a vendor-specific feature, as there is no IEEE standard for multi-chassis aggregation.

CHAPTER 5

Advanced Switch Features

While the common features found on switches are sufficient for the needs of most networks, switches designed for certain networks may provide extra features that are specific to the networks involved. In this chapter, we describe advanced features that may be found in a variety of switches, as well as specialized features found in switches designed for specific networking environments.

Traffic Flow Monitoring

Given that they are providing the infrastructure for switching packets, switches can provide useful management data on traffic flows through your network. By collecting data from multiple switches, or by collecting data at the core switches, you can be provided with views of network traffic that are valuable for monitoring network performance and predicting the growth of traffic and the need for more capacity in your network.

As usual in the networking industry, there are multiple standards and methods for collecting data from switches. In "Simple Network Management Protocol" on page 24, we described one widely-used system called the Simple Network Management Protocol, which can be used to collect packet counts on ports, among other uses. However, while counting packets is useful and can provide valuable traffic graphs, sometimes you want further information on the traffic flowing through your network.

sFlow and Netflow

There have been two systems developed to provide information on traffic flows, called sFlow and Netflow. SFlow is a freely licensed specification for collecting traffic flow information from switches. Netflow is a protocol developed by Cisco Systems for collecting traffic flow information. The Netflow protocol has evolved to become the

Internet Protocol Flow Information Export (IPFIX) protocol, which is being developed as an Internet Engineering Task Force (IETF) protocol standard.

Assuming that your switch supports sFlow, Netflow, or IPFIX, you can collect data on network traffic flows in order to provide visibility into the traffic patterns on your network. The data provided by these protocols can also be used to alert you to unusual traffic flows, including attack traffic that might otherwise not be visible to you.

If your switch does not support traffic flow software, there are still some options available. There are a number of packages that can provide sFlow and Netflow data, using traffic exported from your switch. The traffic is sent to dedicated computers running a software package that turns the traffic from the switch into flow records.

One method used to provide flow data is to "tap" the flows of traffic on the core switch and send the information to an outboard computer running packet flow software. If your switch supports packet mirroring without affecting switch performance, then you could mirror the traffic onto a port and connect that port to the outboard flow analysis computer. If your main network connections are based on fiber optic Ethernet, then another method is to use fiber optic splitters to send a copy of the optical data to an outboard computer for analysis.

Power over Ethernet

Power over Ethernet (PoE) is a standard that provides direct current (DC) electrical power over Ethernet twisted-pair cabling, to operate Ethernet devices at the other end of the cable. For devices with relatively low power requirements, such as wireless access points, VoIP telephones, video cameras, and monitoring devices, PoE can reduce costs by avoiding the need to provide a separate electrical circuit for the device. Switch ports can be equipped to provide PoE, turning a switch into a power management point for network devices.

As you might expect from the name, Power over Ethernet is part of the Ethernet standard. It was developed in the 802.3af supplement and is specified as Clause 33 of the 802.3 standard. The 802.3af version of Clause 33 can provide up to 15.4 watts of DC current over the Ethernet cable. This is the most widely deployed version of the standard. A revision of the PoE standard was developed as part of the 802.3at supplement in 2009, and extends the Clause 33 specifications to provide up to 30 watts.

Many access points, telephones, and video cameras can be powered over the original PoE system that delivers 15 watts. However, newer access points with more electronics, or video cameras with motors for zoom, pan, and tilt functions may draw more wattage. The revision of the PoE standard provides up to 30 watts; some vendors have gone beyond the standard and are providing even higher amounts, up to 60 watts, by sending the DC current over all four pairs of a twisted-pair cable.

While power can be injected into Ethernet cables with an outboard device, a more convenient method is to use the switch port as the *power sourcing equipment*, or PSE. A standard PSE provides approximately 48 volts of direct current power to the *powered device* (PD) through two pairs of twisted-pair cabling. There is also a management protocol that makes it possible for the PD to inform the PSE about its requirements, allowing the PSE to avoid sending unnecessary power over the cable.

With multiple switch ports acting as PSEs, there can be a significant increase in the amount of power required by a given switch. If you plan to use a single switch to provide PoE to many devices, you need to investigate the total power requirements, make sure that the power supply on the switch can handle the load, and check that the electrical circuit that the switch uses is able to provide the amount of current required.

Resources

The following resources may be consulted for further information. Resources are listed here as examples only, and no endorsement of any company or software package is implied.

Resources for Chapter 1

The formal IEEE standards are a moving target: old versions of the standards are periodically updated, and new standards are often being developed.

Bridging Standards

- The specifications for basic Ethernet bridges are found in the 802.1D standard for MAC bridges (*http://bit.ly/ieee-specs*)
- Published IEEE 802.1 "Bridging and Management" standards (*http://bit.ly/ieee-standards*)
- Active and archived projects for the IEEE 802.1 working group (*http://www.ieee802.org/1/*)

Ethernet Standards

- Published IEEE standards for Ethernet (*http://bit.ly/ethernet-standards*)
- Active and archived projects for the IEEE 802.3 working group (*http://www.ieee802.org/3/*)

OSI Model

- The Open Systems Interconnection (OSI) model (*http://en.wikipedia.org/wiki/OSI_model*) describes the set of tasks involved in computer communication as a set of abstraction layers

Ethernet Bridging and the Spanning Tree Protocol

- Cisco IOS Configuration Guide: "Configuring STP and MST" (*http://bit.ly/ZLnZBj*)
- Cisco white paper: "Understanding Multiple Spanning Tree Protocol (802.1s)" (*http://bit.ly/cisco-whitepaper*)
  - This white paper documents the differences between Cisco's version of spanning tree, known as "Per-VLAN Spanning Tree Plus (PVST+)," and the most recent variation of spanning tree developed by the IEEE, known as "Multiple Spanning Tree."
- *Interconnections: Bridges, Routers, Switches and Internetworking Protocols (2nd Edition)* (*http://bit.ly/16m8bcj*), by Radia Perlman. Addison-Wesley. 1999.
  - An expert's insights into network protocols and how networks function, by the developer of the spanning tree protocol. This book reveals how a protocol designer thinks about networks and protocols.
- *The All-New Switch Book: The Complete Guide to LAN Switching Technology* (*http://bit.ly/ZHnARE*), by Rich Seifert and James Edwards. Wiley Publishing Inc. 2008.
  - An exhaustive treatment of LAN switching, from the basics up to the most advanced topics.
- *Routing without tears; Bridging without danger* (*http://bit.ly/15QN4MS*)
  - The inventor of the spanning tree protocol, Radia Perlman, gave this Google Tech Talk in 2008. In the first half of the presentation, she describes how the spanning tree protocol came about and how basic spanning tree functions. The second half of the talk is about a new bridging protocol that she developed called TRILL.

Switch Performance

- Ixia (*http://www.ixiacom.com/*) is a vendor of performance analysis tools whose Web site provides information on how performance is measured. These tools are typically used in large corporate and enterprise networks to monitor and analyze network performance.

- Some tutorials on switch latency specifications and how they are measured, from Cisco (*http://bit.ly/100vWCr*) and Juniper (*http://juni.pr/16JRf0u*).

Resources for Chapter 2

Switch Management

There are many network management packages, and a number of vendors provide some level of network and switch management software for their products. It is impossible to list all of the network management systems, or even a representative sample in these resources.

The packages listed here are examples of network management packages that are not tied to a single vendor or equipment type.

- InterMapper (*http://www.intermapper.com/*) discovers and documents Layer 2 and Layer 3 networks, and includes Netflow analysis.
- NetBrain (*http://www.netbraintech.com/*) network documentation and testing software has the ability to discover and diagram a Layer 2 network:
- SolarWinds (*http://www.solarwinds.com/*) provides a suite of tools that monitor network performance in switches. These tools also use the Simple Network Management Protocol (SNMP) to provide access to interface counters and other switch information.

Resources for Chapter 3

Network design is a large topic, and there are multiple network types that each have different design requirements. Enterprise and campus networks are designed differently than data center networks. Wide area and branch office networks also have their own special requirements. In this section we provide links with information on campus and enterprise network design.

Cisco Validated Design Guides

- Networking vendor Cisco Systems makes available a set of documents (*http://bit.ly/14847xu*) covering "validated designs," which include networking designs for a wide range of network environments. While they feature Cisco equipment, these guides contain a lot of useful information on the topics described.

- One of the design guides that goes into detail on network design is the Campus Network for High Availability Design Guide (*http://bit.ly/14cvCX7*).

Layer 2 Network Failure Modes

All network designs have failure modes. For example, Layer 2 networks are vulnerable to traffic loop failures when spanning tree stops working, or when two ports on a switch with no STP support are connected together. (This happens more often than you might expect. For some reason, people like to play with Ethernet cables.) This failure mode is detailed in these two resources describing the collapse of a large hospital network:

- *All Systems Down* (*http://www.cio.com.au/article/65115/all_systems_down/*)

  — This article in *CIO* magazine documents the failure of a large Layer 2 network design at a major Boston hospital, which forced the staff to revert to paper-based operation while the network was repaired. It's rare to find a useful description of a network failure. Many sites do not publish reports on failures or investigate root causes, and the lack of reports on network failure modes makes this report especially valuable.

- A blog posting entitled *The CareGroup Network Outage* (*http://bit.ly/16fHJAQ*) provides more details on the Layer 2 network failure and "lessons learned."

Resources for Chapter 4

There is a large, worldwide market for Ethernet switches, with many vendors. Each vendor has a product line aimed at a given market or set of markets.

It would be a major task to provide a comprehensive buyer's guide to the Ethernet switch market. Instead, in these resources, we will provide just a few examples, which should not be taken as endorsements of the equipment or the companies.

Switches for the general consumer, and small and medium business:

- Dell (*http://dell.to/YGzmrI*)
- Netgear (*http://www.netgear.com/business/products/switches/*)

Campus, enterprise, data center, and service provider switches:

- Arista (*http://www.aristanetworks.com/*)
- Cisco (*http://www.cisco.com/en/US/products/hw/switches/index.html*)
- Hewlett-Packard (*http://bit.ly/Yz9Ifx*)

- Juniper (*http://www.juniper.net/us/en/products-services/switching/*)

Resources for Chapter 5

Traffic Flow Monitoring

- NetFlow (*http://en.wikipedia.org/wiki/NetFlow*)
- Cisco NetFlow Web portal (*http://bit.ly/106lBVT*)
- Cisco NetFlow white paper (*http://bit.ly/ZwUAM9f*)
- The Internet Protocol Flow Information Export (IPFIX) standard (*http://en.wiki pedia.org/wiki/IPFIX*)
- sFlow Web site (*http://www.sflow.org/index.php*)
- sFlow overview (*http://www.sflow.org/sFlowOverview.pdf*)

Power over Ethernet

- Cisco white paper on PoE and their vendor-specific extensions (*http://bit.ly/ WEj6eo*)
- The Cisco guide to troubleshooting PoE (*http://bit.ly/15rL4uj*) contains useful details on PoE design and operation
- The Wikipedia entry on PoE (*http://en.wikipedia.org/wiki/Power_over_Ethernet*) provides information on PoE operation

Glossary

address

A means of uniquely identifying a device on a network.

broadcast address

The multicast destination address of all ones, defined as the group of all stations on a network. The standard requires that every station must receive and act upon every Ethernet frame whose destination address is all ones.

broadcast domain

The set of all nodes connected in a network that will receive each other's broadcast frames. All Ethernet segments connected with a Layer 2 bridge are in the same broadcast domain. Virtual LANs (VLANs) can be used to establish multiple broadcast domains in an Ethernet system based on switches.

CoS

Class of Service. The IEEE 802.1Q standard provides an extra field in the Ethernet frame to hold both a VLAN identifier and Class of Service tags. The Class of Service tag values are defined in the IEEE 802.1p standard.

Data Link Layer

Layer 2 of the OSI reference model. This layer takes data from the network layer and passes it on to the physical layer. The data link layer is responsible for transmitting and receiving Ethernet frames.

forwarding

The process of moving frames from one port to another in a switch.

forwarding rate

The maximum number of frames that can be forwarded by a switch, typically measured in frames per second.

frame

The fundamental unit of transmission at the data link layer.

full-duplex media

A signal transmission path that can support simultaneous data transmission and reception.

full-duplex mode

A communications method that allows a device to simultaneously send and receive data.

Gigabit Ethernet

A version of Ethernet that operates at 1 billion (1,000,000,000) bits per second.

latency

A measure of the delay experienced in a system. In Ethernet switches, latency is the time required to forward a packet from the input (ingress) port to the output (egress) port.

LACP

Link Aggregation Control Protocol. The IEEE 802.1AX Link Aggregation standard allows multiple parallel Ethernet links to be grouped together, functioning as a single "virtual" channel. A given packet flow over the channel is limited to a single link in the channel; therefore, single packet flows cannot exceed the speed of the individual links. However, multiple packet flows will be distributed across multiple links in the channel, resulting in an aggregate throughput for multiple flows that is the sum of the speeds of the individual links in the group. Link aggregation was first defined in the IEEE 802.3ad standard, and later moved to become IEEE 802.1AX.

link layer

See Data Link Layer.

link segment

Defined in the IEEE 802.3 specifications as a point-to-point segment that connects two—and only two—devices.

MAC

Media Access Control. A protocol defining a set of mechanisms operating at the data link layer of a local area network. The MAC protocol is used to manage access to the communication channel.

MAC address

The 48-bit address used in Ethernet to identify a station interface.

MIB

Management Information Base. A list of manageable objects (counters, etc.) for a given device; used by management applications.

MSTP

Multiple Spanning Tree Protocol. Originally defined in the IEEE 802.1s supplement to the IEEE 802.1Q standard. This version of spanning tree adds the ability for switches supporting VLANs to use multiple spanning trees, providing for traffic belonging to different VLANs to flow over different paths within the network. MSTP is an optional spanning tree protocol that is supported in some switches.

multicast address

A multicast address allows a single Ethernet frame to be received by a group of stations. If the first bit of the destination address transmitted on the Ethernet channel is a one (1), then the address is a multicast address.

NIC

Network Interface Card. Also called an adapter or interface card. The set of electronics that provides a connection between a computer and an Ethernet cable.

OSI

Open Systems Interconnection. A seven-layer reference model for networks, developed by the International Organization for Standardization (ISO). The OSI reference model is a formal method for describing the interlocking sets of networking hardware and software used to provide computer communications over a network.

OUI

Organizationally Unique Identifier. A 24-bit value assigned to an organization by the IEEE. Ethernet vendors use the 24-bit OUI they receive from the IEEE in the process of creating unique 48-bit Ethernet addresses. Each Ethernet device a vendor builds is provided with a unique 48-bit address, whose first 24 bits are composed of the vendor's OUI.

packet

A unit of data exchanged at the network layer.

port

A connection point for a cable. Ethernet switches provide multiple ports for connecting Ethernet devices.

QoS

Quality of Service. QoS is typically achieved by providing different levels of service priority for packet transmission such that, in the event of congestion on a switch port, higher priority packets are served first and lower priority packets are more likely to be dropped. Class of Service bits are used to provide priority tagging on Ethernet frames.

router

A device or process based on Layer 3 network protocols, used to interconnect networks at the network layer.

RSTP

Rapid Spanning Tree Protocol. Initially defined in the 802.1w supplement to the 802.1D standard, RSTP is an improved version of the spanning tree protocol which is interoperable with the classic STP. RSTP provides significantly faster spanning tree convergence in a Layer 2 network composed of Ethernet switches.

segment

An Ethernet media segment is made up of a section of cable for carrying Ethernet signals.

SNMP

Simple Network Management Protocol. A protocol specified by the Internet Engineering Task Force (IETF) for exchanging network management information among network devices and network management stations.

station

A unique, addressable device on a network.

STP

Spanning Tree Protocol. The "classic" spanning tree protocol, defined in the IEEE 802.1D MAC layer bridging standard. The most recent version of the standard, IEEE 802.1D-2004, obsolesced classic STP and replaced it with the Rapid Spanning Tree Protocol.

throughput

The rate at which usable data can be sent over the channel. While an Ethernet channel may operate at 100 or 1000 Mbps, the throughput in terms of usable data will be less, due to the number of bits required for framing and other channel overhead.

topology

The physical or logical layout of a network.

VLAN

Virtual LAN. A method in which a port or set of ports in a switching hub are grouped together and function as a single "virtual" network. All ports within a given VLAN are members of the same broadcast domain.

About the Authors

Charles Spurgeon is a Senior Technology Architect at the University of Texas at Austin, where he works on a campus network that supports over 70,000 users. He has developed and managed large campus networks for many years, beginning at Stanford University. At Stanford, he worked with a group that built the prototype Ethernet routers that became the founding technology for Cisco Systems. Charles, who attended Wesleyan University, lives in Austin, Texas, with his wife, Joann Zimmerman, and their cat Mona.

Joann Zimmerman is a former software engineer with a doctorate in art history. Fluent in tech, academese, and genre, she currently has multiple fantasy novels in progress.

Colophon

The animal on the cover of *Ethernet Switches* is a Common Cuttlefish.

The cover image is from Johnson's Natural History. The cover font is Adobe ITC Garamond. The text font is Adobe Minion Pro; the heading font is Adobe Myriad Condensed; and the code font is Dalton Maag's Ubuntu Mono.

Get even more for your money.

Join the O'Reilly Community, and register the O'Reilly books you own. It's free, and you'll get:

- $4.99 ebook upgrade offer
- 40% upgrade offer on O'Reilly print books
- Membership discounts on books and events
- Free lifetime updates to ebooks and videos
- Multiple ebook formats, DRM FREE
- Participation in the O'Reilly community
- Newsletters
- Account management
- 100% Satisfaction Guarantee

Signing up is easy:

1. Go to: oreilly.com/go/register
2. Create an O'Reilly login.
3. Provide your address.
4. Register your books.

Note: English-language books only

To order books online:
oreilly.com/store

For questions about products or an order:
orders@oreilly.com

To sign up to get topic-specific email announcements and/or news about upcoming books, conferences, special offers, and new technologies:
elists@oreilly.com

For technical questions about book content:
booktech@oreilly.com

To submit new book proposals to our editors:
proposals@oreilly.com

O'Reilly books are available in multiple DRM-free ebook formats. For more information:
oreilly.com/ebooks

O'REILLY®

Spreading the knowledge of innovators   oreilly.com

©2010 O'Reilly Media, Inc. O'Reilly logo is a registered trademark of O'Reilly Media, Inc. 00000

Milton Keynes UK
Ingram Content Group UK Ltd.
UKHW010155260924
448856UK00007B/202